EVANGELINE

AND THE MYSTERIOUS STRANGERS

by Phoebe Hambright Dishman

Dallas: Tuckapaw Media
2015

This collection of essays
is dedicated with love to my parents

Edna Eaheart Hambright

and

James William Hambright

and to my uncle

Paul Robert Hambright

all of blessed memory

Contents

I was going to say that Mother and Daddy taught me to love birds. It would be better to say that Mother and Daddy loved birds. True, they shot some, in their time. Imagine Prescott, Arkansas, in the 1930's. Imagine three boys with .410 shotguns and .22 rifles, stalking songbirds, on the lawn of the Nevada County Courthouse. Imagine that being okay with the sheriff, who sat just across the way, in his office, on the ground floor of the county jail. One of the boys was my dad, the others his brother and cousin.

After the war, Mother and Dad's courtship included fishing on Dallas-area lakes, and other sport, involving guns, and feathered beings. We have the pictures to prove it.

In 1952 my parents moved to Beaumont. Beaumont is a small town in Southeast Texas, near the Louisiana border. In a sense, Beaumont is more Louisiana than Texas. Wrought iron, Spanish moss, scent of magnolia.

Pretty soon I came along, then three siblings. We had a big back yard, with many trees. Always in our den were binoculars, and a Peterson bird guide.

I caught the bird thing, big time. (But not the shooting part.) Long have I loved birds, painted pictures of them, studied their names, observed their behavior.

When Mother and Daddy were in their dying days, my sister and I found an old song in Mother's piano bench, a song which brought a measure of comfort. Verse 1:

> *Still, still with Thee, when purple morning breaketh,*
> *When the bird waketh, and the shadows flee;*

Harriet Beecher Stowe, 1855

"When the bird waketh." Yes, I know that sweet consciousness.

For thirty years I've lived with my husband on a street in Beaumont called Evangeline Lane. Evangeline, with its suggestion of Louisiana, and springing from the Greek word for good news. And so it has proved. We have a small back yard, heaven to me. In that back yard, I have long observed the waking and moving about of Mysterious Strangers, in the guise of birds, and other creatures. "Do not neglect to show hospitality to strangers, for by doing that some have entertained angels without knowing it." One way to entertain angels is to write about them. So in that spirit I offer these essays.

In the world of those who study and write about birds, the rule (fading in some circles) is to capitalize all words in a bird's common name except for a word following a hyphen in a hyphenated name, such as Red-bellied Woodpecker. In the world of those who study and write about mammals, insects, fish, and other life forms, the general rule is to use lowercase letters for such creatures as cats, dogs, squirrels, monarch butterflies, and lizards. But why, some people ask, should birds be assigned greater importance than any other animals? Why, indeed? Other people feel that because, in their opinion, birds and other animals are "things," it would be pretentious to capitalize any of their names, as if they were individuals. To me, birds and other creatures *are* individuals.

Further, my essays are more about a personal relationship with Mystery, and less about a conventionally-aligned conveyance of expert or even general facts. And so, in offering these essays, I was tempted to exercise poetic license and capitalize *all* creature names. But then I thought of you, gentle reader, and elected to capitalize few if any. It flows easier that way. And I

believe the stories afford their own magnitude to the mysterious
strangers. So be it.

> *But now ask the beasts,*
> *and let them teach you;*
> *and the birds of the heavens,*
> *and let them tell you.*

Job 12:7

MOCKINGBIRD NEST

In 1984, when first I saw the charming house for sale on Evangeline Lane, my heart sang. Somehow I knew it would be home, home for Austin and me, for toddler Dave, and my belly round with Robert.

We still love our house. As do the mysterious strangers who frequent its environs.

The mockingbirds, for example. Every year, in the ligustrum bush at the front corner, just outside the window, there's a nest. Usually this process flows smoothly. For the mockingbirds, generation follows generation, an unbroken line.

Nineteen eighty-nine was an unfortunate exception. That year we had a fine, ambitious young cat. Tasha, who was a keen watcher, an expert climber. Tasha, who brought offerings to the back door. Tasha, of the fierce, short life.

Yes, 1989 was a bad year for mockers.

Since then, they've reproduced in peace.

But still they gather their children 'round, and speak, in hushed voices, of Tasha.

This year we were lucky enough to see the whole show. We cheered the parents on as they debated how to place the very first twig. We watched the nest grow. One day there were three blue speckled eggs. Then there were three newborns, blind and helpless. Then their eyes opened, and lo, they were hungry. Three wobbly gray heads popped up, three mouths cheeping for food.

We admired the brave little mother, who covered them during two dark days and nights of torrential rain. When the deluge finally ended, we were sad to see only two babies. This proved temporary; they were sitting on their brother, who in due course reasserted himself. They sprouted miniature feathers. Next thing we knew they were out of the nest, huddled under nearby bushes.

The relatively peaceful nest time was over. But it would be some days before the babies could fly. During this period of on-the-ground exposure, the parents allowed themselves no rest. Each time we stepped outside or even dared to show ourselves at the window, they "chacked" at us.

One afternoon I was sitting quietly on the patio, when father mocker flew down and perched on the chair opposite me. Glaring at me with accusatory eye, he began scolding.

My defense was three-fold:

1. Tasha was indeed a very wicked kitty. But she's been dead fifteen years.
2. Her replacement, Sandy, has no claws. And no ambition.
3. As for me, I wish your children only the best.

After thinking it over, he decided to drop the case against me.

Catbird, First Glimpse

Oh, there's a pretty song in our back yard! One I've not heard before. Sweet, liquid improvisations—like a mockingbird's, only softer, quirkier. I have wondered who this might be. But the songster has stayed out of sight.

Well, yesterday I had my feet up, taking a brief rest before the arrival of company from the other side of the world. Suddenly through the glass I saw a stranger, a dark gray bird with a black cap. He was carrying a twig. He disappeared into the azaleas, to emerge a bit later, sans twig. Another like him joined him on the rim of the birdbath. As he turned to greet her, I perceived a flash of color on his undercarriage, just at the base of his tail. My own mate will testify that I cried out, "He has a red rear end!"

The bird guide puts it more delicately: This bird has "undertail coverts" of robin-red. These coverts are "seldom noticed." That may well be. But *I* noticed.

The bird guide also describes their song. With dawning joy, I put all this together.

The catbirds' scientific name is *Dumetella carolinensis*. I don't hold that against them. Not that they would care if I did. The bird guide also asserts that they skulk in hedgerows. Well, someone has to.

The company arrived. She, I hadn't seen in forty years. She was my friend in high school. He's Australian, which is where they live. Our house was one stop on their long-planned tour of the States, to visit family and see the sights. Long we talked, deep into the night. A glad and grace-filled time.

She brought me a calendar entitled "Unique Australian Wildlife." April's creature, the kookaburra, a bird about whom I was made to sing in grade school:

November's creature, the rainbow lorikeet. A bird whose colors you would have to see to believe. Let's just say it would be impossible for a rainbow lorikeet to skulk in a hedgerow.

CATBIRD, SETTLED IN

I will sing to the Lord as long as I live;
I will sing praise to my God while I have my being.
Let my meditation be pleasing to Him;
as for me, I will be glad in the Lord.

Psalm 104:33-34

Catbirds. They've decided they like our neighborhood. Since Spring began, they've been burbling and mewing like crazy. But I've been unable to find them. No great surprise, for everyone knows that catbirds are a thickety folk. By that I mean they're furtive and skulking. Happy in the hedgerows, dark feathers make concealment easy. Solid gray, black skullcap, long black tail, flipped about with jaunty if secretive air.

How to describe the catbird song, which tantalizes me so? Like their cousins the mockingbirds, they are adept at mimicking the songs of other birds. But not for them the clarion precision of a mocker. No, catbirds are more into improv, that is, rambling riffs of burbles, warbles, squeaks, and chips, interspersed with the catlike mews which give them their name. I hear them at dawn, I hear them at dusk. I am fascinated. I should be content with the music, but I long to see them. For weeks and weeks, I do not.

Until: Late one evening finds me on the patio, snugged into a wrought iron chair, earbuds in, reviewing an emerging mix of sacred song. By some alchemy of weavings from my collection, I find myself growing still. I do not decide to be still. I just am. At that moment, with daylight fading to black, I see a dark gray form on the fence. Another joins it. Be still! Be still!

So still am I that one of the catbird pair, O furtive angel, leaves the safety of the fence and flies to the edge of the fountain not six feet away. There at the fountain the catbird and I are together, with ease.

Next morning, as I'm about my laundry day, a catbird flies down to the grass just outside the back door. Through the glass, he gives me a merry look, and a flip of his slender black tail.

Sunday morning finds me again in my patio corner, enjoying the "hush of nature, newly born." A catbird flies to the birdbath, oh so close. She gives me a bright measured eye, then calmly takes a drink of water. I guess the ice has been broken.

A Rather Belligerent Folk

Something needed mending.

*So I went to the seldom-used room
where my sewing machine is.*

*As I sat at the desk by the window,
arranging the tools of my trade,
reacquainting myself with the machine,
filling the bobbin with the right color thread,
I noticed a slight movement
beyond the glass.*

*Just outside the window,
in the leafy shelter of a large photinia shrub,
was a nest.
In it sat a mockingbird,
she of sleek gray head
and wary eye.*

Ah, I didn't know they nested here.

Their plan, exactly.

I quickly dropped my eyes to my sewing.

*Mockingbirds are a rather belligerent folk,
and I certainly didn't want any trouble.*

Junior Mockingbird

*Oh, for a thousand tongues to sing
my great Redeemer's praise!*

Charles Wesley, 1739

At dark-thirty last night there came a thump outside the window, close to the ground. Then another, followed by a sound of scrabbling. More than a little unnerved, I cracked open the shutters, looked down. On the brick sill outside the glass was a small gray object, which on closer inspection revealed itself to be a junior mockingbird. He was just standing there, on the sill, looking startled. There he was, at that stage I worry over with each summer's new generation: He's out of the nest, but clearly not developed enough to be on his own. Fully feathered, yes, but stubby of wing and tail. Bill lengthening, yes, but broad like a baby's at its base. Strong of leg, yes, but still speckled of breast. And, as a total package, so very small. I wanted to help him, protect him from the night. But, how to contain a wild youngster? How to feed him? Plus I had a feeling that given the irascible nature of mockingbirds, he would very much resist capture. So, to help him, to protect him from the night, I got down on the carpet and blessed him through the glass, giving him the gift of my full benevolent attention, my swelling heart, for whatever that was worth. Then I closed the shutters.

Opening the shutters again at first light, I saw he was gone. Oh dear. Ah, but wait! I went out to get the newspaper and there he was, perched atop the ground cover by the front door. I went for my camera. He let me get very, very close. From several angles, I captured the wonder of him. All the while, his parents scolded me from the elm branches above.

Studying the images, son Dave noted that the little guy had his chest puffed out, as if to let the world know who's a big bad bird. I was heartened by the implications of this perspective, that is, that here was a germ of scrappiness ready to be introduced into a world of hazard. Bring it on, world! But feed me a little breakfast first, if you please. Perhaps a nice pre-tenderized lizard. Yes, I would like that very much.

Grow up scrappy, little bird. Grow up strong. Learn many songs. Make it your business to express them. Live up to your name: *Mimus polyglottos*. Mimic of many tongues! "Oh, for a thousand tongues to sing my great Redeemer's praise." I wonder if that phrase came to Charles Wesley when first he visited the New World and met a mockingbird.

Thrashing Away

After a long cold winter, our backyard is coming to life. A little weedy and worse for the wear, yes, but green, with splashes of color—roses red, azaleas pink and white. Although they've not yet bloomed, the amaryllis shoots are thrusting up.

To enhance the chlorophyllic emergings, there's warm-blooded activity:

Birdsong brings joy, the squirrels, comic relief.

Reptilian stirrings, too: The green lizards are awake. I had the dubious pleasure the other day of seeing one bring down and eat a bi-plane (one of those big awkward mosquito-looking creatures.)

Speaking of birds, the brown thrasher is back. Yesterday marked my first awareness of his return. There he was under the azaleas, elegant in his chestnut coat and streakéd vest.

Golden eyes aflame, he was "thrashing" in the leaf-debris.

I suppose this energetic and rather alarming-looking flailing is to scare up a worm. If I were a worm, I would dig in deeper and wait for the thrasher to go away.

Brown Thrasher and Its Allies

I was weeding the flowerbed the other morning, minding my own business, when I looked up to see a beautiful brown thrasher, not ten feet away. Evidently it was searching for food to feed a hidden offspring—I could hear a low cheep or two from the wax myrtle. When the adult saw me, it froze. Then it began scolding. I backed ever so slowly away from that long curved beak and preternaturally yellow eye, remembering the time a territorial blue jay created a new part in my dad's hair.

Later that day the brown thrasher, aware of my watching presence inside the house, made a militant show for me, sharpening its beak on our new cedar fence.

And only moments ago, not even daylight yet, there came a "thump" at the window by my computer. Glancing up in some alarm I saw a long-legged speckle-breasted brown bird scuttling away, across the pavement. I considered myself warned.

Speaking of bird strangeness, do you know the ghost dove? More scientifically known as Eurasian collared-dove, this monolith of pale concrete gray hangs around the yard, occasionally browbeating the listener with a kind of strangled passive-aggressive complaint: "I called and called… pick UP, you!"

Eventually it gives up and flies away, with a grunt like a laryngitical crow.

Then there's the mockingbird, who hurls itself over and over at its reflection in the glass. (When it first started performing this strange ritual some weary weeks ago, we thought someone was knocking at the back door.) Now and then while winging home with a tasty worm it remembers about the "bird in the glass" and interrupts its homeward flight to flutter down and strike a blow or two for the cause. It does this with worm still gripped in its beak, which transfers worm-essence to the window, which makes more work for me. Sigh.

Guess birds and people alike are just trying to work out their lives and manage the best they can. There seems to me to be a lot of mutual incomprehension.

Brown Bird on the Patio

"Phoebe, what's that bird on the patio?"

"It's a brown thrasher, dear."

Our casual tone belied our great interest in this bird. Shape in the shadows, flick of brown disappearing—seldom does a thrasher emerge from the deep cover of thicket and hedgerow.

To see him so close to our window, lit up by the morning sun—graceful incarnation of rich chestnut, white wing bars, heavily striped breast, long tail, golden eyes—what a gift for the two humans on whose patio he perched!

Of course, other brown birds live in our yard. Ah, those chattering, oh-so-numerous ones, the house sparrows. I suppose they're a gift, too. In their way.

I know every bird of the mountains,
and everything that moves in the field is Mine.

Psalm 50:11

House Sparrow

Housebound as I am with a remodeling project, I cannot escape their infernal racket. Heretofore the little wretches have mounted their attack on my nerves strictly from the back yard. Now the sparrows have kicked it up a notch, sending an agent within my very walls.

How he got in, heaven only knows. I follow the ear-splitting chirps to their source. He dives behind a bag of grout. I drag him forth, and lo—he's just a fledgling fluff ball, little more than a baby.

My enemy, transformed.

With care I release him to his kinfolks outside. And so, by opening my eyes to what it is I hold in my hands, by redefining "neighbor," God inches me a little closer to the practice of radical hospitality.

> *Therefore you are to be perfect,*
> *as your heavenly Father is perfect.*

If God can love a sparrow, maybe I can, too.

Asilomar Song Sparrow

One morning in Pacific Grove, California,
my friend Kathryn and I rose from our beds,
drank coffee in front of a cozy fire,
then reported to the Pacific Ocean
for our pre-breakfast constitutional.
A dawn patrol, if you will.

In the sand at our feet,
in the shrubs and grasses of the dunes,
out over the sea, vast and wide,
in the radiant sky above it,
many wonders we saw.
As we swung vigorously along the boardwalk
in our sturdy athletic shoes, our hearts were light.
And if the California gulls
patrolling above us
heard two contralto voices singing certain verses
of certain old songs of the church,
"Love lifted me,"
"When the roll is called up yonder…"
so much the better.
God's breath in our nostrils, and the world was new.
How could we keep from singing?

On my person I carried a folder,
an illustrated list of birds we might observe.
We had studied this folder in advance.
Wherever my friend and I go, you see,
whatever meets our gaze,
be it power lines, or Monterey pines,

we keep an eye trained for feathered friends.
Such friends we find in vermilion flycatcher,
swallow-tailed kite, roseate spoonbill —
well, why not?
Birds, we believe,
are among God's most special angels.

So this day on the Pacific
we were wending our way back
from the ocean toward the dining hall,
our hunger rising with the sun
but eyes and breath still trained,
which was a good thing,
for in a shrub by the boardwalk
we suddenly saw and heard
a bird.
So close we could have touched him.
Not that he would have allowed it.
One's physical person is sacred, or ought to be.

Just a small brown bird.

Maybe so, but he had his head thrown back,
his nostrils full of God's breath,
and he was singing like he owned the place.
Singing brisk and bright, such an outpouring,
a flow welling up, to bless the earth.
And no wonder, for a look at my list confirmed
he was none other than a song sparrow,
Melospiza melodia.
Melodia. There's within my heart a melody,
so how can I keep from singing?

He's a pretty creature, the song sparrow,
with breast strongly streaked,
and a little upturn of the mouth
that looks for all the world like a smile.
And why not smile?
To be in that place, by the Pacific,
in the soft-grass dunes,
in a pleasant shrub, God's breath in his nostrils.
And so he smiled, he sang, he trilled,
he made his offering
to the new day.

And my friend and I,
the breath of God in our nostrils,
the wonder of this tiny creature in our hearts,
came a little more alive,
grew a little deeper and richer in our love
for this earth-home of ours,
our gratitude
for the time we have to work and play here.

CARDINAL MANEUVERS

Awake, my soul, and with the sun
Thy daily stage of duty run;
Shake off dull sloth, and joyful rise,
To pay thy morning sacrifice.

Thomas Ken, 1674

The stage of duty this summer morning was our patio, where the morning sacrifice paid by Rusty the Brittany spaniel was to submit more or less philosophically to shampoo, water hose, and his implacable owner, who as usual stood on his leash to keep him fully present in the moment.

Another family had shaken off sloth and joyfully risen—I could hear baby northern cardinals chirping for their breakfast. Their father appeared, with an unidentifiable but no doubt tasty tidbit in his beak. The trouble was, he saw me watching. So there ensued an amusing series of maneuvers designed to confuse me and keep the location of his babies hidden. After a moment or two, I had mercy on him, lowered my eyes discreetly so he could deliver the breakfast in peace. Sure enough, the plaintive chirping stopped, and I was so happy, that the cardinal was a diligent parent, that Rusty was clean, and that we were all at least for this morning full and safe. Amen.

Praise God from whom all blessings flow,
Praise Him, all creatures here below;
Praise Him above, ye heavenly host;
Praise Father, Son, and Holy Ghost.

Thomas Ken, 1674

To a Redbird, Near My Window

Even the sparrow has found a home, and the swallow a nest for herself in which to set her young, near Your altar, O Lord of hosts, my King and my God. Happy are those who dwell in Your house; they forever praise You.

Psalm 84:4-5

Mama cardinal has built a nest, just outside my window, approximately three feet from this computer. I can see why the angel wing jasmine attracted her: good cover, and pretty, too. Glossy green leaves, fragrant white flowers. And there's a sheltering eave above. Still, it's remarkable she would build so close to humans. I have a feeling she's been sizing us up a long time. As I work at my desk I can see her bright black eye looking at me through a little triangular space in the leaves. I have heard her singing softly on the nest. Yesterday (Mothers' Day!) I saw her mate bring her a seed, place it gently in her beak. I like having her so close. Still, I know the dangers ahead. For one thing, we have a boisterous family of blue jays this year. Jays have been known to steal eggs and chicks from other birds. My eye is closely upon them…

Redbird Lady on your nest,
Coral lipstick, feathered crest,
Close to me you choose to dwell;
Your mate is singing like a bell

Of Cheer! Cheer! And you reply,
Sweet and soft, with shining eye,
Of Life, to which you give your best
Of eggs beneath your feathered breast.

I know you know I'm watching you;
It gives you pause what I might do.
Brave and tender Mother's heart,
Eternal watching is our art.

Each day holds hazard, sad but true;
I'll help you watch, I'll pray for you.

CARDINAL NEST

Days pass and the years vanish, and we walk sightless among miracles. Lord, fill our eyes with seeing and our minds with knowing: let there be moments when your Presence, like lightning, illumines the darkness in which we walk. Help us to see, wherever we gaze, that the bush burns unconsumed. And we, clay touched by God, will reach out for holiness, and exclaim in wonder: How filled with awe is this place, and we did not know it! Blessed is the Eternal One, the holy God!

Gates of Prayer

What's with all the gray? On assessing the weather one recent morning, my husband pronounced it "dingy." I agreed. I looked out to the birdfeeder for the consolation of a little color. But all I saw was gray. Two squirrels, two mourning doves, half a dozen white-winged doves: gray, gray, gray.

Suddenly, a bolt of electric blue—jaybird! All heck broke loose. Appearing from somewhere offstage, where she'd been touching up her coral lipstick, mama cardinal zipped back to her nest in the angel wing jasmine. Daddy cardinal unleashed crimson wrath on the jay. Jay sprang up from under the feeder and zoomed away. Red-bellied woodpecker joined the fracas, scattering the smaller birds...

For a few moments, it was pretty colorful. Then, we lapsed back into gray... set to the dingy twitterings of a host of house sparrows. They're not gray, but they might as well be.

So I'm watching mama cardinal on her nest, when suddenly she draws up, looking kind of startled. She peers below her, settles back down. Hmmm.

Next morning, still gray. But behold! By some intuitive timing I climb up to stand on the computer desk, from which vantage I peer down through the glass into the nest, just in time to see neonates Rachel and Richard Redbird wetly struggling out of their shells. Now they are two blind, silent, wide-open mouths. Mama and Daddy spring into action, bringing formula. This goes on the rest of the day. Mama seems okay with my surveillance. Daddy, on the other hand, having spent little time around the nest until now, is understandably skittish of me on the other side of the window. But, my presence must be borne.

This morning finds Rachel and Richard Redbird still wobbly, but bigger and stronger. I see one of them stretching tiny wings. And what's this? Now there are three! Is it that you, Rhonda? I am transported. Daddy is hovering midair, giving me an Ungentle Look. Day by day I watch the babies grow. Then I have to go out of town…

Sad news: just home, to an empty nest. We knew the low survival rate for baby cardinals. We knew the hazard posed to them by blue jays and squirrels. But the blow came from an unexpected direction: *Corvus brachyrhynchos*. The crow did drop one baby, which was preserved for my brokenhearted inspection. What perfection he was. I could be cynical, gray, over all this. But there is another choice.

Cardinal Trainees

Earlier this summer I reported to you some sad news—that Mama and Daddy Redbird had lost three babies to a wicked crow. I come now with glad news: Mama and Daddy tried again. The fruit of their hope: two redbird trainees—a boy, and a girl. Such a twittering, such a chirping! Such a testing of wings!

This morning I met the boy face to face, through the glass of a window into which he'd just crashed. He's pretty indeterminate-looking—mostly brown. No swashbuckling mask. Not yet. And so he looks rather tentative, rather blank.

But his crimson color is taking hold. His flight feathers and tail feathers are long and strong.

There he perched, just past the glass, on a wrought iron chair. As he pulled himself together, he eyed me this way and that, practicing the Look his father is so fond of giving those not of his tribe.

Later, I crept as close as I could to the Myrtle Grove, in which the whole family was gathered: Mama, Daddy, Boy, and Girl. Overhead, the three sacred trees. Understory: roses, periwinkles, pink indigo, amaryllis, holly fern. In this Eden the little family was hopping about, enjoying the cool of the morning.

On the patio, in the angel wing jasmine, I saw another trainee—a lizard so young he was neither green nor brown, nor any particular color at all. So very small was he, less than two inches. But mighty. Or so he thought. He waited, he lurked, he grabbed a small white moth. Alas, even a small moth proved too much of a mouthful. It escaped. But the lizard is learning. Give him time.

Mechanical Redbird

You pushed me violently so that I was falling,
  but the Lord helped me.
The Lord is my strength and my song,
  and he has become my salvation.

Psalm 118:13-14

No spark for the work at hand, I drooped at my desk. Seems like only yesterday I was singing along sunlit paths. So what am I doing in this black pit today? Who pushed me?

Where is my strength and my song?

Where is my strength and my song? Well, as they say, from our mouths to God's ear! A flash of color, just outside the window. I carefully turned my eyes. Sure enough, a male northern cardinal had swooped down to perch on the back of a patio chair. Vivid drop of purest crimson, chirping merrily, swiveling this way and that as if to captivate, as if to refresh. Bright-winged messenger from God.

That was how I chose to see this bit of grace. As it turned out, this redbird's particular message was aimed at someone else, someone just offstage—someone to whom he was giving detailed instructions.

You have seen how I made my approach, quoth he. How I judged the distance, how I landed so surely and gracefully. You have seen how I did it. So now, if you please, do thou likewise.

Right on cue, aiming for the back of another chair, a young redbird-in-training swooped down to join its father. I'm sorry to report it overshot the target. There were painful consequences. Painful, as in a pane of glass.

Oh, Father, cried the child, that bird in the glass pushed me violently, and made me fall down! The father's wordless gaze signaled only this: Remember who you are. So the youngster pulled itself together and fluttered up to the chair.

I say "it", because though fully grown in size, the distinctive male or female color had yet to appear. Its feathers were a somber shade of brown, its beak as black as the tiny metaphorical cloud over its head.

After a reflective moment or two, the daddy flew away. The youngster remained, meditating no doubt on its brief, tragic life. We've all been there, have we not? Sadly, worse was to come.

A forceful flurry of gray exploded onto the scene, struck our wretched redbird with malice aforethought, and dashed it to the ground. Seems a mockingbird needed that chair.

Hey, you big bully! You pushed me! Too bad, Junior, that's life.

I didn't know whether to laugh, or to cry. But the scene stayed with me.

Later that day, I received an email from my friend Melissa, who lives in another city. Now, Melissa is a journalist, a person who keeps a close eye on current events. In that spirit, her message to me was as follows:

"Run, don't walk, to Walgreen's, and look for the mechanical birds." That was all she wrote. Layers of whimsy and grace! Show me a sign for good! My full strength returning, I headed to Walgreen's.

By the time I got there, real clouds had rolled in. Hideous, menacing, indigo clouds, with strange flashes and rumblings, with the scent of brimstone around the edges. Seems not one but two storms had met on a street corner in the sky over Dowlen Road and Folsom Drive.

Things were about to turn ugly. Just as I made it in the automatic door, all heck broke loose. Howling wind, claps of thunder, buckets of rain.

But I didn't care, for stacked in display just inside, like a feast for my soul, were dozens of mechanical birds. Several were singing, each in its own language.

There were blue jays, goldfinches, robins, yellow warblers, eastern bluebirds, and, sure enough, vivid drops of crimson. Bright daddy redbirds.

Now, these birds had been crafted so carefully that they transcended their medium, which was, of course, plastic. Cradled in boxes designed to look like sunlit aspen forests, blessed with the inspired name "Bird Songs in Motion," gifted by Cornell Lab of Ornithology with species-specific birdcalls, correct in posture and profile, focused, alert. Each bird sealed with the invitation to "TRY ME!"

With permission, I called forth one of the redbirds from its box, for inspection. I found that what animated him was a little electrical eye sunk into his breast, such that any motion he detected would set him off into raptures of pretty, pretty, pretty, and cheer, cheer, cheer.

He put his whole body into it, his whole mechanical being. As he sang, he gestured decisively with head and tail. He had a kind of nervous tic, interspersing his song with a strange and wonderful clicking noise. When he finished what he had to say, he closed his red beak firmly.

How could I resist? Soon I had a redbird in a sack, and Walgreens had ten of my dollars, plus tax. Simple pleasures for simple minds, and who's to say it wasn't gas and money well spent?

The storm finally abated. I left Walgreen's with my treasure. He sits now on a shelf by my desk, at eye level. All I have to do is make a move, and he springs to life, clattering, clicking, chirping the good news that I'm free free free to cheer cheer cheer my world and make it as pretty pretty pretty as I can.

So I bought him a blue jay for company. And such a blue jay! But that's another story.

16

Blue Jay

When we were clearing Uncle Paul's house, which had been our grandparents' house before it was his, I found my grandmother Ruth's guide to the birds. Tucked inside, a one-page article, brittle with age.

The title: "Don't Gainsay the Blue Jay."

The subtitle: "This blue blusterer may offend your ears, but there are other sides to the story."

The article begins:

> People often look at the bad side of Blue Jays because they make noise, quarrel, rob nests, attack cats, and lack humility. But there are finer sides to their personality— besides being beautiful, of course. For one, they are the sentinels of bird-dom. When they set up a shriek all the other birds know a hawk or your cat is nearby.
>
> And if the hawk or cat keeps coming, the Jays will close ranks and attack. Many a Robin or songster owes its life to warrior Blue Jays.

Oh how thrilled I was to find this. I knew our grandmother loved cardinals. But her affinity for blue jays, evidenced by her saving this item, was news to me.

Warrior jays, those "handsome haughty creatures." The blue team. Shrieking, quarreling, scrabbling on my roof. See them transform the birdbath into showers of diamonds. Hear them whispering to their babies.

Here's my conclusion:

If a jay can rise with every dawn
and take up his duty on my back lawn,
if he can fit a bandit's mask
to full embrace of heaven's task
and love his Creator with all his might,

with all his shadow, and all his light,
if a jay be nimble, and brave and strong,
and ready to say when he is wrong,
if he can stand in the gap and shriek,
if he can help the mild and weak,
if he can narrow those bold black eyes
and get in some licks before he dies,
well, give me a jolt of electric blue
and let me be a jaybird too!

17

MERLIN

*Behold, I am doing a new thing; even now it is springing to light.
Do you not perceive it?*

Isaiah 43:19

I have always loved that verse from the prophet Isaiah. I may be a little dull of perception, but sometimes I get the sense that God is up to something. Sooner or later, if I pay careful attention, He will bring it to light. Perhaps.

In the meantime, what He wants from me is a still heart—and busy hands.

Take my new sanctuary for instance. It's like this—my eldest has left to go to college. I miss him. But every cloud has at least one silver lining! A young man has gone forth to try his wings. That's good, that's the natural order of things. *And*, a spare bedroom is now mine, all mine.

David had hardly reached Savannah last week when I felt the strangest compulsion to claim my new space. My husband and younger son rolled their eyes and got out of the way. Several groaning garbage cans, trips to Goodwill, and mementos laid reverently in storage boxes later, I had my sanctuary. A place of beauty, order, simplicity. Harmonious furnishings and objects—not one thing more or less than needed to be there.

I didn't buy anything new, just rearranged the old and special. Embroidered pillowcases from my trousseau, never used before, ready now should a guest or beloved son come for a visit. A cheerful quilt with squares of blue and white, made by my husband's grandmother, mounted on the wall to cover the worst of the nail holes. My girlhood dresser. An "antique" copper fan. A desk, set in a window—a beat-up desk, true, but plenty of space for projects. A little stack of seashells from my father. A clear, round paperweight from my mother.

This may sound strange, but there's a kind of holy hush in that room now, and I cannot help but think that God was in the whirlwind of clearing and cleaning, and now God is in the silence.

"Behold," God says, "I am doing a new thing; even now it is springing to light. Do you not perceive it?"

Do you ever feel what some have called "holy unease," when your hands are flying away at your daily tasks, but there is something making you restless, expectant, maybe even a little apprehensive?

So I'm at my "new" desk, working away, glancing up now and then to admire the view out the window. Nothing extraordinary. Just a dense green thicket of red-tip photinias, as high as the window, screening me from our neighbors' driveway, sheltering an air conditioning compressor.

Did you know that *photinia* is from the Greek word for "light"? The house sparrows gather in this green, lit-up world, amusing me with their animated conversation, sometimes hopping onto the windowsill, then withdrawing in alarm when they perceive my presence just beyond the glass. Simple pleasures!

Yes, I am content, but I am also alert. The mark of a good sanctuary, I think, is that it affords a peace that is active, not passive. A peace that keeps you on your toes. Jesus tells us over and over to stay alert, which I am in this place, which is a good thing, because, suddenly, there she is.

With a swoop of her powerful wings she scatters the flock of sparrows. As my jaw drops, she lights on top of the air compressor, in plain view, and regards me with a fierce brown eye, ringed with gold.

She is compact, no bigger than a blue jay. But the hooked beak and powerful talons tell their story. She is a raptor, a bird of prey. My mind scans the field training my dad gave his children—she is small, she is brown, she seems to be hunting sparrows—could she be a sparrow hawk? Yes, she could. But she isn't.

She ruffles her feathers, spreads her tail just long enough for me to get the full effect of the elegant bars, and then she is gone.

Five minutes later, as I sit there still stunned, she makes another pass through the photinias and lands, again, on the air compressor. She is real. She is offering the miracle of another chance to absorb her markings. "Do you not perceive it?" she seems to ask.

She takes off again. This time she's really gone. But I have seen her. Really seen her. She is imprinted on me, forever. I race for the birdbook, and my heart stops when I see what she is: merlin. Miniature falcon. In medieval times they called her lady-hawk. Why? Because if you were a lady in need of a hawk, that is, if you were an outdoor kind of girl, fond of hunting, you had a merlin. Dashing, fearless, strong. But small and gentle enough for a lady to handle.

The word "merlin" means "courageous." That, she is. Courageous, independent, and very good at what she does. She moves through space as if there were absolutely no time to waste. She hunts with lightning speed, using three methods: determined and deadly chasing, power dives at up to 200 hundred miles per hour, and surprise attacks from inconspicuous perches. A lady to be reckoned with!

I say lady, for the one who visited me was female. As I mentioned earlier, she was brown, the males being gray, or powder blue.

These days, merlins are seldom seen. One reason is their relative scarcity. Another reason: "Merlins are often overlooked by bird watchers because of their tremendous speed. They appear and disappear before anyone can say merlin."

Yes. My enchantress was the mere blink of an eye. Two moments of pure joy, one to introduce herself, and one to make sure I understood the gift. That was all.

Fierce, wild creature, in an unexpected place. What if I had missed her?

18

American Goldfinch

Winter each year brings swarms of American goldfinches to southeast Texas. Males and females, dressed alike, in their cool-weather garb of olive drab. Massed at the feeder and on the ground below, undifferentiated, yet each individual so tiny, so quick, with their little black wings.

As winter wears on toward spring, the males begin to put on their courting plumage. Just a hint of gold, usually, is all we in the South get to see. Now and then, though, a lit-up lemondrop. Thrilling! A grace note vouchsafed, all the more precious for its rarity.

And then one day the flock is gone, headed up north to their breeding grounds. Up north, for the full display of gold.

In the woods this weekend, at the retreat center, spring was in full song: northern cardinals, blue jays, Carolina chickadees, Carolina wrens, red-bellied woodpeckers, pileated woodpeckers, mockingbirds, mourning doves.

First prize for volume went to the cardinals with their "what-cheer cheer cheer," "birdy birdy birdy," etc. Such elated clarion courting, from predawn to after dark, competed mightily with my "silent retreat." Ah well, spring will have its way.

Final grace note: There's a mockingbird trilling in my backyard right now, pre-dawn. He knows many songs, which he strings together delightfully. My favorite: a sprightly wolf whistle, repeated three times.

19

Coldfinch

If a brother or sister is without clothing and in need of daily food, and one of you says to them, "Go in peace, be warmed and filled," and yet you do not give them what is necessary for their body, what use is that?

James 2:15-16

No sooner had I commenced my exertion on the elliptical machine this frigid morning, the better to keep myself physically fit and thus more response-able to whatever the unfolding day might require, than my attention was caught by a situation "beyond the glass." On a branch of the Chinese elm, four American goldfinches, puffed up, hunkered down, forlornly eyeing the empty birdfeeder.

Ah yes, it has been "too cold" the past couple of days for me to fill the feeder. I wanted to, I really did. But I never quite got out there to do it. And now I'm busy with something else, for the theoretical common good.

Yet here sit four actual "brothers and sisters," hungry.

Should I help them now? Do you think they could wait thirty minutes for me to finish my exercise?

Well, the Divine Teacher raised amused eyebrows at my questions, and showed me the next thing: Having despaired of the feeder, the goldfinches flew down to the birdbath. They tapped their beaks around the edges of the frozen water. One ventured out onto the ice, hoping for a thin place that might yield to his pecking. All in vain …

Okay, okay, I get it! In a trice I was bundled up, on the patio, addressing the ice with the handle of a wooden spoon. But the ice was solid. It would not yield. I turned next to the hose, to add some water on top of the frozen mass. But the water in the hose was frozen. So I brought a pitcher of water from the house, poured it on top of the ice. Then I filled the feeder.

No sooner was I back in my warm house on the elliptical than the goldfinches were into the seed and onto the birdbath, sipping the fast-freezing (but not yet frozen) water. And I was thinking of my mother, of blessed memory, who as an aspect of nurturing her four children gave us bird books, and bibles.

20

WREN SONG

He wakens me morning by morning, wakens my ear to listen, like one being taught.

Isaiah 50:4

The dawn was drowsy, steamy with golden light. I was at the mailbox posting a letter, when the quiet came alive with song. I was instantly alert, every nerve stretched. Ah, the birding game, and I must play!

Having read about his distinctive chant, I suspected who the songster might be. But I wanted to know for sure. So I crept up the driveway to a certain reverberating magnolia tree.

Broad glossy leaves completely hid the source of the music. Behind his wall of green he must have sensed my scrutiny, for his song suddenly ceased. Wary silence, then an outraged buzz: *zhwee zhwee zhwee!* Suddenly a wee brown bird broke cover and winged toward the pear tree in the backyard.

I could now say with assurance, "There goes a Carolina wren."

Another ID this week, first by song – a low, clear *peter peter peter*. Must be a tufted titmouse. (To my delight, the birdbook lists titmice under "Chickadees and Their Allies." Who would not want to be friends with a chickadee?)

But wait, be careful, let's have a look. Ah, there he is, and he is indeed a tufted titmouse. But not just any. He's a variation—a *black-crested* tufted titmouse!

What a thrill to listen, watch, and make connections. Like one being taught.

21

Yellow-rumped Warbler
(The Artist formerly known as Myrtle Warbler)

'Tis February. Bleak midwinter, cheerless gray,
and you are busy, inside the house.
Not too busy, though, to glance out the window.
Drab and dreary, little to see. Just me.
Nondescript, gray like the day.
Just a small gray bird, perched in the fog on a fence.
Just a small gray bird.
But you, looking at me with narrowed eyes,
I can tell you're a woman trained, trained for possibilities.
Just as you begin to turn away,
I execute a charming adjustment, a nimble turn…
Oh good, the game is afoot!
You move quickly for your field glasses, praying I'll stay.
I do. Not for you, of course.
Where else but your fence would I watch for insects?
Be that as it may, I stay.
And when you train your glasses on me:
black mask, bright eye, yellow spot on my crown.
But the thing that makes you mine, Valentine,
is the blazing sunshine just above my tail.
They say I'm the most visible warbler.
They say this is because I perch with my golden rump-patch
"outrageously exposed."
Exposed, perhaps, for those with eyes to see!
At any rate, the radiance of my tiny presence
(12.3 grams, to be precise) pierces your heart.
That is my way.

22

CONFUSING FALL WARBLER

This morning in the backyard I saw a small, sprightly embodiment of Life. Feathered, of course, for such draws my eye. Black cap, yellow belly, green back and tail. And did he have a white cheek? Can't be sure.

He flirted with me, zipping from branch to branch of the azalea.

I searched the bird book in vain. Did you know there's a whole section on "Confusing Fall Warblers"?

Sat down to write about him, and lo, he appeared on the angel wing jasmine, just outside my window. Another chance to identify him.

But I was so transported by his cuteness, so wrapped up in calling him precious and darling, that before I knew it, he was gone. Again.

Maybe the point was that I love him, not own him.

Someone has said that love brushes past us in little moments such as these.

Other times, love goes winging past in formation. Yesterday morning, in the western sky, I saw three large pink birds traveling together to whatever mission field was their aim for the day.

Roseate spoonbills? Most likely. I seriously doubt they were flamingoes. Again, they were mine to glimpse, not own.

23

Bell's Vireo

We've been graced this winter by a pair of red-shouldered hawks. Their occasional appearance on utility pole or back fence is exhilarating, to say the least. With their fierce aspect and magnificent markings, how beautiful they are.

There's also been activity in the hedgerows below. The usual suspects: northern cardinals, house sparrows, confusing warblers. Recently among them, a small gray stranger.

He keeps a low profile. We think he might be a vireo. According to the dictionary, vireo comes from the Latin *virēre*: "to be green." As Kermit the Frog says, it's not easy being green. Especially if you're gray.

Turning to the bird guide, we learn that he's a Bell's vireo, described unflatteringly as "perhaps the most nondescript vireo."

The guide says further that he sings "a husky, unmusical song … as if through clenched teeth."

Nondescript, unmusical, afflicted by lockjaw—he deserves credit for singing at all!

I had the field glasses on him this week as he perched in the pineapple guava, when who should hop into the picture but a ruby-crowned kinglet. So much for the vireo's moment of fame. I could almost see his jaw clenching in irritation. For a ruby-crowned kinglet—with its tiny cuteness, wing-flirting ways, and brilliant red crown spot—is bound to steal the show.

Oh well. As the psalmist says, "Trust in the Most High, and seek goodness; live harmoniously upon the earth in peace, and with assurance" (Nan Merrill's paraphrase of Psalm 37:3-4).

Be your nondescript self, little Bell's vireo. Be yourself, with assurance. After all, with hawks above, perhaps one does not want to flirt cutely about with a bright red target on top of one's head.

24

HUMMINGBIRD

I was working in the back yard, when there fell upon my ears the most hideous buzzing, from within the garage. It sounded like Godzilla the hornet. It sounded like a miniature jackhammer, cranked up to warp speed. The noise was so intriguingly horrific that I decided to master my fear and discover the cause. So I crept in, straining to see without being seen. I needn't have bothered with stealth, though. She was way too busy to notice me.

The setting: We're inside a standard double garage, with a standard garage door, open, as it usually was in that more innocent day. There's also a single garage door at the back, always closed. Across the top of this door, a row of clear glass panes.

Well, a little jewel of a ruby-throated hummingbird had mistaken one of those panes for a shortcut through the garage to the garden beyond. Her plan inexplicably frustrated, she was attacking the glass with all her might. A full frontal assault. So intent was she that I was able to walk right up to her, my heart pounding with the wonder of being so close. After I admired her furious perseverance for a moment or two, I reached out and cupped her in my hands. A miracle!

Naturally *she* did not view it as a miracle. Talk about a bad day; now a giant had her. After she got over the shock of that, she was *really* mad. Trapped inside my two hands, she still had a mighty weapon: her voice. Her long beak protruding through the space between my thumbs, she gave me the full benefit of what was on her mind. She poured forth speech. In what the bird-book rightly calls a high, petulant tone, she commanded me to let her go. So I her obedient servant carried her out to the driveway, opened my hands, and let her go. As she zoomed away, she delivered herself of a few parting remarks. Then she was gone.

She was gone. Likely she never gave the event another thought. But I did. I thought, what a wonder to have this pugnacious particle, this wisp of life, in my hands. Her life, in my hands.

The secret every hummingbird should know is that someone is watching her, someone who cares very much for this miniature manifestation of His will. Every beat of her fierce little heart, every hum of her gauzy wings, every hard journey across the Gulf to her wintering ground and back, every summer storm as she shelters her little clutch of eggs, every sun-drenched morning she works the flowers in the back yard, her Creator is with her. From the day she hatches to the day she perches for her last sleep, her Creator is with her. Truly, God knows every iridescent feather on her hard little head.

Civilla D. Martin, 1905

25

CHICKADEE, RESURRECTED

I was very busy, preparing the house for company. Amidst the whirl, I decided to go out to the curb and check the mailbox. Strange, this detour, for mail was the last thing on my mind. Still, something called me in that direction. I opened the front door. From the Chinese elm I heard a clear whistle, which sounded strangely like my name. In vain I scanned the tree for the songster. Then I stepped out the door. Ah. At my feet, on the mat, a Carolina chickadee, feet up. Evidently he had flown into the glass beside the door and knocked himself out.

I picked him up. In my hand he lay, so small, four inches long at most. His eyes were closed. His chest heaved, his beak opened and closed in shock. However, his neck seemed okay. So perhaps there was hope.

Out the front sidewalk I carried the little fellow. He could help me get the mail. But there wasn't any. I remembered that it was a holiday. Back up the sidewalk, into the house, feather weight in my hand.

I sat on the sun porch, holding him, touching the softness of black cap and bib, white cheeks and belly, uncurling the miniature feet, stretching out the perfection of tiny wings.

Suddenly, in the sanctuary of my hand, a quickening. A bright eye opened. He looked up at my face. As the clouds cleared in his little brain, he began to take inventory, run a scan of his systems. I took him outside, sat down in a chair on the patio, and continued to watch. Still on his back, resting in my hand, he gazed up at me, turning his head this way and that to get a better look. Suddenly, still in my hand, he flipped from his back to his feet. He hopped from my hand to the edge of the iron table. For a moment he regarded me, without fear. Then he zoomed away, up into the Chinese elm.

As a fitting close to this interlude, I consulted the bird book, which describes Carolina chickadees as "small tame acrobats." That, they are. Under "voice," a surprise. I had supposed that all they said was "chickadee-dee-dee-dee." Well, it seems they have another note, a call, a clear-whistled "fee-bee." "Fee-bee."

And now, when I hear a chickadee, or see one, I wonder if it's the one I held. Or his mate perhaps, she who could not lift her beloved out of harm's way, so she called my name.

26

Chickadee Request

Early this morning, as I was trying to wake up and get the kitchen going, a Carolina chickadee announced that the bird-feeder was empty. He may be tiny, he may be outside, but the buzzing of his voice certainly carries.

Am I tuned to chickadees, in particular? Could be, as I've held a stunned chickadee in my hand, so warm and vulnerable and small. And then the quickening, the revival! Such moments tend to create new communities.

Anyway, at the dear little loudmouth's request, I filled the tube with sunflower seeds. As soon as the word spread, trouble began. Such a jostling for a place at the table. It must be said that the main bullies are the white-winged doves. But the chickadees wait around the edges, and eventually they get what they need.

Going the extra mile: Glancing out the front window the other day, I saw a *Trachemys scripta elegans*, otherwise known as red-eared slider turtle, high-stepping westward across our yard. By its size, roughly a foot long, I knew it was a she-turtle, ancient of days. Did you know they can live thirty years?

I went outside to greet her. She pulled smartly into her shell. But after awhile, she stretched out her elegantly scripted neck and looked at me. I asked her why it was that she who is "chiefly aquatic" was traversing my bone-dry St. Augustine grass. She said nothing. I tried asking her about the healed-over crack on one side of her shell. Again, she kept her counsel.

I thought briefly of managing her destiny by putting her in the fenced back yard with a pan of water. But I decided to live and let live. Blessings on thee, Lady Turtle. Blessings on your journey.

I cannot close without sharing that my son Robert's first full sentence was spoken in response to seeing a red-eared slider turtle in our back yard. He burst into the kitchen with news of great joy: "Turtle walk, ou'side!"

Robert's first full sentence happened, oh, a quarter century ago. Could the turtle today be the same one? If so, her name is Turtis (rhymes with Curtis), for so Robert's older brother David named that long-ago creature.

Where have the years gone? Why is our yard a turtle-path? A turtle-path to where?

27

A Sparkle of Chickadees

For they have refreshed my spirit and yours.

1 Corinthians 16:18a

Black caps,
black bibs,
white cheeks,
flurry of tiny wings…

What are they doing??

Seems this morning
the sun-kissed shrubs
are rich
with raindrops

and the Carolina chickadees,
leaving the birdbath
to more traditionally-inclined folk,
have decided to bathe
on top of the hedge.

The sparkle of their play
does me good.

28

CHICKADEE: HOLY CONVERSATION

65

I was wandering around the backyard in my bare feet, ankle-deep in rain-fresh grass, portable phone to ear, engaged in long-distance conversation with a friend, who was laying out a situation for which she needed me to pray.

Because of my intense focus on her, I was less aware than usual of the beauty around me.

Suddenly I woke to the reality that I was standing less than three feet from a Carolina chickadee. We were, in fact, eye to eye.

He was perched expectantly on the (empty) birdfeeder. Having caught my attention, he eased into the conversation, holding forth at some length in chickadee language, whether in friendly greeting or demand for seeds, who knows?

I reported his presence to my heavy-hearted friend on the other end of the line, and she, a fellow bird-lover, chortled with glee.

For both of us, something shifted.

29

American Robin

Just at first light, or a little before,
comes a caroling.

Sweet notes, simple and pure.

Not the ardent "cheer!" of the cardinal.

Nor the jubilation of the jay, that blue bandit.

Not the mocker, whose repertoire this year
includes an especially fine "Chickadee-dee-dee,"
and the name of an author I admire:
"Gurd-JEEF!"

No, here is the robin,
"a very familiar bird;
recognized by its gray back
and brick-red breast."

American robin, sturdy fellow.
Commonly seen on grassy lawns.
Not too forward, not too shy.

In song, just a few short phrases, rising and falling.
Just a few sweet notes, simple and pure—
and robin has delivered his message.

Beyond that, he has little to say.

But all day long, his hard work speaks for him.

"Work, for the night is falling!"

I take his message, and try to apply it.

30

EARTHWORM BLUES

The torrential rains brought to our back sidewalk an earthworm, an earthworm so long that had it not been for his squishy locomotion I would have thought him a snake.

After a close perusal of his person, for the sake of science, I felt compelled to address him:

"Friend, I'm afraid you've made a tactical error."

The problem (his problem, anyway) is that we've had a bumper crop of American robins this year. Robins with keen eyes, and hearty appetites.

I felt that no matter how waterlogged his wormhole, he should have stayed in it.

Sure enough, not long after I went inside, I heard a *Turdus migratorius* trilling a merry "Thank you."

Poor worm.

Family of house sparrows, chirping monotonously at the feeder. Typical scene, all too comfortably familiar. Just as I was glazing over, a Stranger blew into town.

In configuration I would call him a sport model. Like a sport model, he moved fast. Zip in, snag a seed, zoom away. So it was hard to get a clear picture.

But each time he zipped in, I made it my business to snag another detail. As I watched, a pattern slumbering in my brain came to life; I "knew" he was a nuthatch.

Research revealed him to be not just any nuthatch, but a red-breasted nuthatch. *Sitta canadensis.* What a glorious little fellow! Slate blue above. Orange belly below. Abbreviated tail. (Bird guide says "stubby." Would you call the back-end of a Corvette "stubby"?)

As to his adorable sleek head: black crown. Below the crown, a neat white racing stripe. Below the white racing stripe, a brisk black eye-stripe, extending into a long bill. In the upward curve of the bill, a hint of mirth. Oh yes, birds can smile!

His mate joined him, she of paler belly and bluish crown. But just as smiling, just as zippy.

I hear that nuthatches can climb a tree-trunk head down, using their strong legs and feet, feeding on insects they find in the bark. From the energetic acrobatics of this pair, I would not be surprised.

As to the nuthatch voice, their call is reputed to be "a weak, nasal *ink* or *yenk*." To this I cannot testify. But I would expect them to have more of a "vrrroooom."

32

SHRIKE

Two creatures came to my attention this week.

First, on the power line above our back fence, a bird I've not seen in our yard in twenty years. (My not seeing him doesn't mean he hasn't been here.) In the rain, stoically perched, a loggerhead shrike, aka "butcher bird."

Can you imagine a songbird of the predatory persuasion, with strong bill cruelly hooked, for killing and dismembering prey? That is the essence of shrike. But all I see on the power line is a stolid fellow, gray and white, with a black mask.

True, it's a rather ferocious-looking mask.

Shrike. Like unto a mockingbird, but with shorter legs. In further contrast to a mocker, who flashes about with alert expression and mobile tail, the shrike sits quite still, with an appearance rather on the heavy-headed side.

There is another difference. You know the mocker's song: quick, accomplished, attitudinal. The shrike's song, on the other hand, consists of "halfhearted notes and phrases, deliberate, with long pauses…"

I consulted Webster for the etymology of "shrike." To my delight, I found that "shrike" is akin to Middle English "shriken," which means, "to shriek."

Here, clearly, is a creature who wants to let loose with a shout, but who is constrained by something like a headache.

Take courage, shrike! You may yet shift the Universe, by the thoughtful, quiet expression of who you are.

Who are you, anyway? Can it be true you are Vlad the Impaler? (Shrikes are inclined to "store" their prey for future consumption by hanging them on thorns or other sharp objects… Aren't you glad you asked?)

The second creature I found in the garage. This small fellow's breath had been taken away, but he was not yet dust. No, in his pose he looked still alive, if in a rather darkened and desiccated state. Here was the mummy of a green lizard, hanging upside down from a windowsill, by one tiny claw of his back foot. As if he were still running. What could this mean? Blessings on thee, small one, now returned to your Source.

33

GOATSUCKER

When I saw him, in a tree,
This is what occurred to me:

In naming birds, there's deviation
'Twixt Latin and English appellation.

Caprimulgus, musical name.
Goatsucker, though, a bit of a shame.

His English name seems provocation;
Does he deserve such defamation?

'Tis bad enough to look like him,
Pressed down, dusky, on a limb.
Head like an anvil, feet so feckless,
Whiskery bill, gaping reckless.

"Cryptically colored," like forest debris,
Spotted and spooky he looks to me.

Beyond "goatsucker," his group-umbrella,
A particular name has this odd fella:

"Chuck-will's-widow"—can it get more off?

Yes, it can.
For when he's not going on and on
about poor Chuck-will's widow,
Or flitting nocturnally through the woods,
gulping bugs,

He's inclined to mutter,

"Grof, grof, grof."

I can attest, because, you see,
He gave a number of "grofs" to me.

34

Mourning Dove

Be ye therefore wise as serpents, and harmless as doves.

Matthew 10:16

Doves, harmless? Could there be, at times, a twinkle of mischief in those bright, staring eyes? I can testify they found creative ways to tease and bait our Brittany spaniel Rusty (he of blessed memory.) Seems there are more brains in those sleek little feathered heads than you would think.

Once I spied a mourning dove in our back yard. Nothing unusual, to see one there. Before the overwhelming advent of white-wing doves, mourning doves were numerous in our neighborhood. I saw them often, perched on power lines, stepping daintily across the grass. Sprinkling of black spots on slender gray-brown body. Long pointed tail. Whistle of wings on takeoff. And often I heard the mournful hooting that gives them their name.

This mourning dove was working at a particular task. He seemed to be taking the measure of various small twigs. I watched through field glasses as he hefted different possibilities. With each, he performed a kind of baton-twirling routine. Some were too big, others awkwardly shaped. But some were acceptable; he flew off with the chosen.

Sure enough, a flimsy platform began to appear on a branch of the magnolia tree just outside our kitchen window.

Darkness lifted, sky brightened in the east—I looked out, and there she was, Mrs. Mourning Dove, warm breast spread over their future offspring.

35

COME, HOLY GHOST

This afternoon, 'neath the Bill Lee Memorial Birdfeeder, a flurry of activity. Chattering, elbowing, shoving … The American goldfinches are tiny eating machines, plumping up for the trip north to their breeding grounds. The house finches are competing with the goldfinches, spurred on by their aggressively rose-breasted tribal leader. Northern cardinals zip in and out of the fray. A white-winged dove stalks about on legs of vivid red. In an icy puddle, Sam the house sparrow shows off for Susie, sending up a spray of diamonds.

So I'm ellipticalling away, listening on my earbuds to love-wrecked Mark Chestnut wishing for wings to help him rise above Time and get past the pain, when into the confusion under the birdfeeder drops the Holy Ghost.

Well, not the real Holy Ghost. Unless one wants to get metaphorical. What it really is, is a Eurasian collared-dove. Compared to other doves they are intimidatingly big, and their color is a gray so preternaturally pale that my Uncle Paul was pleased to call them ghost doves. Which whimsical name thrills me no end.

Rest in peace, Uncle Paul. With your smile and the arch of an eyebrow, with your jewel-like observations laid out for my cherishing, you have sharpened my eye for the road. And the back yard.

36

White-winged Prayer

I know every bird of the mountains,
and everything that moves in the field is Mine.

Psalm 50:11

It was Easter afternoon. For the creatures in my back yard, just another day. I watched a squirrel belly-crawling toward the sunflower seeds in the grass under the feeder. I assume the belly crawl was a stealth-tactic, or perhaps a gesture of submission, designed to deflect the potential wrath of the large blue jay already feeding there. When the jay saw the squirrel approaching, he did bristle a bit. But he decided to share the space, and the food.

Later I saw a squirrel drinking oh-so-warily from the birdbath, one solemn bright eye watching, watching, watching for danger. It's a danger-dance out there. In addition to the touchy backyard regulars, there are hawks.

That same Easter afternoon, I was on Pinchback Lane with my husband and one son, poking about in an empty house. Aim: to see if the house should stand and be repaired, or go. It was pretty bad. We were on the ground floor when I spied a bird, who had somehow found her way inside and gotten herself trapped. She sat on a windowsill, looking longingly at the great freedom beyond the glass. Our son reported he'd seen her yesterday and tried to shoo her out, but she wouldn't leave.

Well, I've encountered birds in her predicament before. I knew what to do. I walked up to her and took her firmly in my hands. After a brief struggle (may those two tail feathers grow back!) she surrendered. A young white-winged dove. Small for her species, not fully mature. Her body heat, and the frightened beating of her heart, were striking.

Took her outside, opened my hands. And lo, she spread her wings and flew.

House finches. He, with sparrow-like features, dashingly dipped in red. She, with sparrow-like features, marked by "drab streaks" and "weak face pattern." Hmmm.

Today a male house finch bullied his way onto the feeder, shoving aside a female. It seems that Dashing trumps Drab and Weak. But before I could cry "Gender domination!" another female lit into the male.

Before I could cry "Serves you right!" the male flew with his sunflower seed to a junior house finch, and fed it.

Just so. There are reasons. I should keep watching.

Another thing to observe is my strong disapproval of white-winged doves.

I can't help it. There are too many of them, and they dominate the smaller birds, and they suck down the seed in the bird-feeder before anyone else can get to it. And so I call them "birds of low character." As if judging their "goodness" or "badness" will change anything! Still, it makes me feel better.

Yesterday morning, one smacked into the back door. This they do with irritating frequency, leaving dusty prints on the glass.

Instead of flying off, as they usually do, this one fell to the ground. I went out to see about it. It rose to its little red feet and ran from me.

But then it slowed, and wobbled, and sank to the concrete. I reached down, picked it up. Its weight, warm in my hand. After a feeble effort to peck me, it relaxed, laid back its little head. I petted its soft silver breast until its eyes closed. It was gone.

After a time of silence, I stretched out one perfect wing, loving the contrast: wing patch white, flight feathers dark.

Beautiful creature, in my hand.

38

ANOTHER DOVE DOWN

Heal me, O Lord, for my bones are dismayed.

Psalm 6:2b

At the breakfast table, we're discussing an item in the morning news: Beaumont police officer, killed in the line of duty. Terrible photograph, of a crumpled car.

As we absorb the shock, there comes a mighty "whomp" against the back door. Not unusual: White-winged doves are swarming this summer, and once or twice a week one mistakes our glass for a throughway.

They're a tough breed, *Zenaida asiatica*. Seldom is any harm done—by the time we arrive at the scene of the impact, all we see is a dusty body-print, perhaps a tiny breast-feather or two.

This time, though, a dove is down. He lies hunched forward, beak on the pavement, eyes opening and closing. There he remains, long enough for us to suspect he's badly hurt. But I can see by the slight lift of his head that his neck is not broken.

We go outside; I pick him up. The warm roundness of him in my hand is both blessing and bad sign.

His eyes are russet, surrounded by feather-rings of iridescent blue. After admiring him, stroking him, which truly is all the aid we can afford him, we put him back on the patio, breast down. He slumps forward again, where he remains, growing more and more still. His eyes close. He's gone.

Five minutes, ten...

I remember years ago, when I fell off a footbridge. Ten feet, onto the hard creek bed below. After impact there was no breath. And deep silence. Then, awareness of a stunned circle of loved ones, looking down at me. Then, my body gathering itself, commencing a computer scan, to see if I was still a viable entity.

Then, sound and breath rushed back—and there was pain. Oh yes I'm alive all right!

So it is for the dove. Inventory complete, his breath returns, and he stands up. Gingerly, he walks away from us, toward the grass. We follow, cheering him on, imagining his embarrassed cover-up: "It's cool, baby." We get too close; he takes wobbly wing up into the Chinese elm.

He's probably out there right now, in the crowd under the feeder, shouldering his compadres out of his way.

39

RED-BELLIED WOODPECKERS

Do you ever worry about his neck?
I'm referring, of course,
to the male red-bellied woodpecker.
For him, for all within earshot,
the dawn comes up like thunder.
Thunderous strafing.
Furious fusillade, on the metal gutter.
Does this behavior seem a little crazy to you?
It does to me.
I can only conclude the earsplitting racket
is to impress a potential mate.

(I'm remembering the school dances of my day,
the crowd falling back reverently
for the requisite "drum solo,"
couples drawing closer...)

Wooed, and won.
Our red-bellied woodpeckers make a fine pair.
Together they bully our birdfeeder
with rude shoving, and trills of maniacal laughter.

You can tell the male from the female.
His cap of iridescent scarlet
extends from nape of neck to base of bill.
Hers, nape only.

And those necks! Rock-solid, resolute.
Oh ye doves, of slender, pliable neck,
you with your mincing ways,

clear out, begone!
We need that seed!

For the woodpeckers have produced a child.
He is cute,
in a nondescript kind of way.
As he flutters about, learning to fly,
he looks a little surprised to be here,
a little unsure what to do.
He does, however, show promise
of a sturdy neck.
The way a woodpecker is designed to be.

40

MISSISSIPPI KITES

Fortune favors the prepared.

So it was that when I was invited to go on a field trip with the Big Boys and Girls of Birding, aka the Golden Triangle Audubon Society, I hastened to a sporting goods store. There I selected a "breathable" khaki outfit—shirt and pants, each with myriad pockets, tabs, loops, other utility features. I also bought a khaki sunhat.

Then I went to the hunting section where I picked out the *pièce d'résistance*, a "large waist pack," with room for field glasses, pencil and paper, insect repellant, bandana, battery-operated fan, all the accouterment ensemble (as I imagined it) of an experienced birder.

So the big morning came, and I donned all this gear, plus khaki-colored clogs. The effect was not altogether what I had hoped. Oh well, too late. If I was Jane Hathaway in Jackie O sunglasses, so be it.

The trip was a success. I kept up with my betters, who charitably made no comment on my outfit. (What could they say?)

And, I saw my first Mississippi kite. On beholding him high above, I cried out that surely it was a crow! I was gently corrected.

It must be told that the day was uncomfortably warm. And so was I. The Jackie O sunglasses, hermetically sealed as they were by their rims to my sweating face, produced a fog. The breathable outfit was not. And, if you ever need to "lose inches fast" and don't feel like buying one of those sauna belts, you are welcome to borrow my "large waist pack." Be warned, however, that it's impossible to access its contents expeditiously. When you unzip it, all the contents fall out. I'm not sure why. Nevertheless…

It was a good trip. And lo, less than a week later, I was walking up my own driveway, when what should I see highsoaring above Major Drive but two Mississippi kites, *Ictinia mississippiensis*.

Running inside for the field glasses, I ran back out and trained them on the heavens and experienced such joy, not just in the birds themselves, lovely as they are, but in knowing their names.

41

Swallow-tailed Kite

I was at the stop sign, pondering the busy day I was about to engage, when beauty swooped in and dashed the to-do list out of my hand. Metaphorically speaking!

Grace sublime, gliding low, just above the green stand of pines on the other side of Major Drive. Four-foot wingspan. Upper body dark gray, verging on black. Exquisite head and undercarriage, white as snow.

I shook off the shock, engaged my bird lore. Bald eagle? Not big enough. Pterodactyl? Not likely...

Then it registered: Look at those elegant wings outflung. Look at that tail, vigorous V for Victory. Look at the heart-stopping buoyancy of his flight. Here we have *Elanoides forficatus*: swallow-tailed kite!

I had heard of them. Seeing was believing.

Resembling very large falcons, swallow-tailed kites live mostly in the South. They prefer a scattering of trees, the edges of woods. They are extraordinarily graceful, entirely beneficial and "becoming scarce." A "highly aerial species," they hunt for small creatures in treetops—lizards, for instance—and for airborne insects, such as grasshoppers. And lately, they've been seen above Beaumont. Most recently, by me.

When I shared news of the sighting with my siblings, one of them indicated, oh, a little skepticism.

But then one Saturday we were all in one car when we spotted an *Elanoides forficatus* swooping over the intersection of Delaware Street and Lucas Drive. More witnesses, more believers.

Perhaps you'll see a swallow-tailed kite one day. If you do, try not to drive off the road.

42

Goshawk and Its Kind

My friend and former high school classmate is a professor at Perkins School of Theology. The other day, he spotted Something atop the steeple of Perkins Chapel. It was perched on the cross. Knowing my affinity for Somethings, he snapped a picture and emailed it to me.

Well, my bird guide pretty much falls open to the hawk-pages, so it was quick work to reply to him that the Perkins percher was none other than a male northern goshawk, *Accipiter gentilis*. Or so I believe. Beautiful bird: pale gray below, dark gray above, with a black bandit-mask over which there's a dashing white stripe. Such a stripe is called a "supercilium." (Same root as supercilious: "Haughty eyebrow." Now you know!)

If I'm right, the goshawk was out of its range. My bird guide says that "sightings of accipiters are often very distant, or very brief…" Rare appearance, by a haughty-eyebrowed bird.

Seeing such a rarity, through Ted's eyes, atop a sacred place, against the clear blue of a Dallas sky, comes mighty close to heaven. How the raptors thrill my heart! Thank you, Ted. "Forest Park, our ideal school, always faithful we will be!"

Another hawk-story: One morning last week I spotted a visitor perched in the Chinese elm. A very large visitor. It was an enormous red-shouldered hawk, head tucked, enjoying a nap. Never have I seen a hawk asleep!

Not for long. Perceiving my presence, up came that magnificent head, fixing its stern gaze upon me. He shook his feathers, and took off.

And I, I grinned from ear to ear.

The Hawk is more than he appears to be. Everything is.

"The Spirit bloweth wild, high-surging where it will…"

43

Give Me a Raptor

Fake out!

How many times have I hurried to the window, enticed by the cry of a red-shouldered hawk, only to find a blue jay at his expert mimickry?

What is the jay's motive? Why pretend to be what he is not? Why not stick to "Jay, jay, jay"?

Or that delightful signature song, beloved by my sister Barbara and me:

"Beeeeedleeyoop!"

(The birdbook claims that the jay's sweet-whistled song is "toolili." That is just wrong…)

Blue jays are nice, in a bold if unsettling way. But give me a raptor!

The other early morning I was on the patio, watering my plants. On my cheek, breath of a breeze. On my head, the sun. What could be better?

Suddenly o'ershaded, I looked up. Behold, a red-shouldered hawk, cutting silent circles in the sky.

"How silently, how silently the wondrous gift is given!"

Round and round wheeled the hawk, with no discernible aim. Sturdy wings outflung, handsome tail-bars spread—ah, he was not alone! His mate appeared, cutting circles of her own.

And then, behold, another entity—fruit of their union. Yes, a hawk-child! As he reeled and wheeled, I saw him turn his head, checking in with Ma and Pa.

With each hawk, my heart sprang higher.

44

BALD EAGLE

The young eaglet from Sooner Lake, whose progress has been beamed all over the world via "nest cam," is eleven weeks old today. I continue to check on him/her from time to time. How fascinating, what a blessing, to have seen him grow from a tiny gray fuzz ball, helpless, to the strapping adolescent he is today.

He spends less and less time in the bowl of the nest. He perches at the outer edges, or hops up onto the manmade beams that support the nest. He flexes and flaps his mighty bald eagle wings, as if to say, "What are these strange, magnificent, promising things attached to me? What am I to do with them?"

I think he'll figure it out before long, for his parents are gradually reducing his food-allowance. His first flight will be soon, very soon. Perhaps even today.

Come Josephine, in my flying machine
Going up, she goes! Up she goes!
Balance yourself like a bird on a beam
In the air she goes; there she goes!

Alfred Bryan, 1910

45

BUZZARDS AND THEIR ALLIES

You've heard of San Juan de Capistrano,
how the mission bells ring and the chapel choirs sing
as the cliff swallows wing their way home?

Oh yearning heart, oh tender sigh, oh misty eye…
Graceful creatures, home each year
on St. Joseph's Day, March nineteenth,
to the cliffs of California.
"That's the day you promised to come home to me." Sniff.

Lesser-known fact: Each year, on March fifteenth
(beware the Ides of March…)
the turkey vultures come home to Hinckley, Ohio.
Turkey vultures, also known as buzzards.
Evocative name, yes?

The townsfolk of Hinckley gather at dawn,
scanning the skies over beautiful Lake Hinckley,
whose high rock ridges are the beau ideal for buzzard nesting.

Once the buzzards show up, as they always do,
Hinckley starts the party.
Music, pancakes, storytelling…Good times!

In Cherokee lore, turkey vultures
are called "peace eagles," because they don't kill.
Maybe not, but up close they look a little troubling.
Shoulders hunched, small red faces
with staring brown eyes,
huge nostrils, wrinkled foreheads,

beaks of ghostly white.
Unlovely on the ground,
struggling awkwardly for liftoff…
Still, once aloft, they possess a certain grace,
soaring for hours on thermal updrafts.

Their feeding habits are what they are.
Their Latin name Cathartes *translates, "purifier."*
A good thing.

Hinckley loves them.

How do turkey vultures know when it's March fifteenth?
They don't say.
Even if they wanted to say, they couldn't.
Having no voice box,
their only comment is a grunt,
or, if pressed harder,
a truly scary hissssss.

I heard of the buzzard homecoming from Mr. Griffith,
my high school biology teacher.
This news got my attention, for March fifteenth is my birthday.
Perhaps one year I'll make a pilgrimage to Hinckley.

Or, perhaps not.

Mid-March this year did find me in the heartland—
Hillsboro, Kansas, to be precise.
As my mother might say, Kansas in March is cold as a frog.
Dark sky heavy with sleet and snow.
The farmhouse is snug and warm.
Sensible girls would stay in, by the fireplace.
But oh, there's a gift waiting,

a gift for which three friends must venture out.

The gift is bald eagles.
Bald eagles in bare trees, posted around the perimeter
of Marion Reservoir.
Twelve regal statues, watching for ripples in the icy water.

The eagles watched the water, and we watched them.
Now and then we'd see a liftoff, a seven-foot wingspread.
Now and then we'd see a swoop, as fish became food.

Oh the eagles take your breath away.
Sable feathers, snow white heads and tails.
Aristocratic beaks, talons of disconcerting potential.
And oh, those yellow eyes—fierce like the sun.

Not above a little opportunism, true. Even a little roadkill.
And I hate to tell you,
but they don't scream like in the movies.
Like their buzzard cousins, they squeak, and grunt.
But unlike their cousins, they're gorgeous.
So ferociously gorgeous.

We visited them on two consecutive days.
The second day, March fifteenth,
something extraordinary happened.
Some kind of invisible signal passed among them.
As we watched,
one eagle lifted from its branch, drifted skyward,
describing lazy circles upward.
Then another lifted, then another, till all were circling.
Round and round they flew, higher and higher they spiraled,
till they were tiny specks above.

Who declared this upward adventure?

Eventually the bald eagles spiraled down again,
and settled back to their posts.
And then, scores of snowy white pelicans,
having caught the eagle-spirit,
arose from the chilly water,
from the bleak islands,
and forming two large groups
made their own double-spiral statement of joy
in the gray March sky.

Marion Reservoir — place of deep wisdom.
The birds were about fishing, about the duties of survival.
But there was more.
Some secret signal, and suddenly
they were about the sheer gladness of being alive.

And they soared, cutting circles in the sky.
And they jostled each other, playing games.

And their joy lifted hearts below.

I dedicate this essay to Mike Griffith, who modeled a keen appreciation of creation. He was strict, and highly engaging. (Oh those blue eyes!) There were, however, students inclined to watch the clock on the wall above his head. One day we arrived to find he had cut a circle of black paper and taped it over the clock, calling it a permanent eclipse. Dr. Michael E. Griffith, killed with 23 others in Killeen, Texas, October 16, 1991. He had changed his schedule to be at Luby's Cafeteria for an early lunch, to counsel a friend in need.

Black Buzzard at Lake Travis

What a pretty scene.
Our room is at ground level—
were I to lean over the balcony rail,
I could almost touch
the native grasses,
the steep downward slope of indigenous shrubs,
at the foot of which, far below, stand
cedars, at waters' edge, with sun on their heads.
Then Lake Travis, stretching silver across
to boat slips and buildings,
and green hills beyond.
In the blue above, feathery clouds.

Framing the foreground,
an oak tree,
graceful and tall.

Beautiful, this vibrant stillness.
Butterflies work the wildflowers—
swallowtails, monarchs.
Flash of redbirds, he through the cedars,
she investigating lit-up lantanas.
Flash of grackle, very close—
iridescence, beat of wings.
Time slows, like honey…

We're drawn to honey, aren't we?

"And Samson turned off the path
to look at the carcass of the lion.

And he found that a swarm of bees
had made some honey in the carcass.
He scooped some of the honey
into his hands
and ate it along the way..."

Carcass? Did someone say carcass?

With no warning at all,
he's flying straight for my face.
His aim, evidently, the balcony rail.
Just in time he sees me,
veers for the nearby oak,
in which he crash-lands
with stunning force.

The oak and I absorb the impact.

The oak has seen him before,
and I have seen one like him,
startled, bursting like a bat out Hades,
from a sleepy old barn in Kansas.

That time like to gave me a heart attack.
This time is worse.

I recover, somewhat.
The tree branch steadies
to support its new load.

And what a load.
A vision of loveliness he's not.
Who is he?

Two feet tall in his stocking feet,
with a wingspread of five,
he's Coragyps atratus.
Black vulture.
Pale gray legs has he,
supporting a hulk of a body covered
in rusty black feathers.
Stubby tail has he,
shoulders hunched,
dark snake of a neck.

And his face? Well …

I know. He can't help it.
Besides, his mother loves that cute little face.
But even among vultures, he's a shady character.

Some black buzzards,
stressed by overpopulation,
have grown too hungry to wait for their prey to die.
Tempted by newborn calves and such,
they have become
buzzards behaving badly.

So there stands an alleged miscreant,
on whose villainous visage I do not care to look.
And here sit I, determined to keep my place.
What is the reconcile to this impasse?

I decide to embrace the discipline of close attention.
Though it makes me ill to look at him,
surely it won't be for long.
Oh really?

As if reading my thoughts, he settles down for a siesta.

The good news is,
once he draws in that naked neck,
once those pale legs disappear under the bulk of his breast,
he doesn't look quite so bad.

He rests.
But now and then
his periscope goes up—
perhaps something has died!

A half-hour passes, very slowly.
I will not vacate the balcony;
he will not leave the tree.

Finally the impasse is broken:
From a distance, far down the shore,
a laugh rings out.
A high, piercing, Ricky Ricardo kind of laugh.
I laugh, too.

So does the vulture.
Well, not out loud, for he has no voice box.
But he does open and close his beak,
his version of a wink and a smile.
Could a buzzard and I have the same silly sense of humor?
Seems so.

Refreshed, he stands and stretches.
Then he takes to the air.

I should say, rather,
that he falls heavily out of the tree,

evidently on purpose.

His angels bear him up.
Circling, he glides close to me,
feathered fingers outstretched
in farewell.

Then he flaps away, out over the lake.
He becomes a dot in the distance.
Then he is gone.

Hallelujah.

The wind heaves a sigh of relief,
and so do I.
The oak tree dances
for joy.

Thus ends my close encounter
with the dark side.

47

GRACKLE INVASION

*My friend reports
that her back yard was invaded the other day
by a flock of boat-tailed grackles.*

*They had heard about a bowl of cat chow
on the back step.*

*Feeding grackles was not what my friend had in mind
when she placed it there.
Nevertheless …*

*For this treat, the grackles formed a line,
or as the British would say,
they queued up.*

*My friend stands witness
that when it came his or her turn,
each grackle would step up to the bowl,
take one unit of cat chow,
then report to the back of the line to wait for another turn.*

*There were a couple of skirmishes.
But in general,
decent order prevailed
until the bowl was empty.*

*Having heard this story,
I'm more favorably inclined
toward grackles
than I used to be.*

I'm still troubled
by their numbers,
their staring yellow eyes,
the stormy brown of the female,
the unearthly iridescence of the male,
the unabashed pursuing on every roadside,
the cacophony of their ear-splitting conversation,
the product of their mass roosting on the hood of my car.

But I do thank them
for the demonstration
that with a spirit of respect and cooperation,
there can be enough cat chow for all.

48

Yellow-billed Cuckoo

She mentioned the matter in Sunday School.

A name laid out, for my consideration:
"yellow-billed cuckoo."

The next Sunday, she mentioned it again.
This time I jumped on it.
We agreed to seize the day.

At three that afternoon,
she picked me up, and we drove to the Sabine Woods.
Sabine Woods, where a certain Visitor has been reported.

Once there, we spent two hours
exploring mystic shadows and sunny glades.
There was a light breeze. But the sun did not move.

The butterflies were numerous and lovely.
But their startling colors, their ragged flight,
proved a little distracting, a little confusing.

The trees were lush from recent rains.
But here and there, trunks were spun in ghostly shrouds,
and strange brown fungi grew at their feet.

At the edge of a clearing we saw a rabbit.
His ears, huge ovals, translucent.
But his gaze was not the gaze of a rabbit.
The eyes meeting ours were bold, unafraid.

Wildflowers nodded along the paths.
Turk's cap, trumpet vine.
Poppieeeess…
Okay, there aren't any poppies in Sabine Woods.
But we did feel rather drugged.

Perhaps it was the heat, the blending of our sweat
with Deep Woods Off.
But I think it was mostly the spell
of the yellow-billed cuckoo.
He who moves furtively through dense foliage,
in search of tasty insects.
Again and again he called,
with his guttural hard knocking: tok tok tok.
Invisible, just out of reach, luring us on.
Finally, rewarding our perseverance,
he gave us a glimpse.
He posed for us.
A slender bird, twelve inches long.
Dark upperside, white belly and throat.
As advertised, his bill is mostly yellow.
And lining his long black tail: bold white spots.
Like unto planets, hanging on the cheek of the night.

49

SWANS

Anahuac Wildlife Refuge:

Among the wonders that day, a female vermilion flycatcher,
she of mild dark eyes.

Complementing her flitting about for insects,
with dips "like a phoebe,"
were several interludes of perching,
as if to allow us a good look.

We found her to be more vividly colored
than the bird book illustration.
We found her to be charming.

Our bird list grew long.
And yet, the wonder we came for eluded us.
Three hours, four hours, five…
Light fading, time to go home.

One last stop, Shoveler's Pond.
Does it get more spectacular than the bold pattern,
the orange eye, the white "bridle," the emerald crest,
of a male wood duck?
Why, yes it does!

"Something" on the far side of the pond caught our eye.
A pair of large Somethings, snow white, with dark masks.
Behold, the tundra swans!
They of recent rare appearance in our area.
They whom we sought.

The bird book is pleased
to call them "short-necked and gooselike."

We found their necks to be graceful, enchanting,
perfectly designed to win our hearts.
As we watched, as twilight deepened,
one tundra swan stretched its neck upward,
pointing toward heaven.

A good day. Yes.

50

BROWN PELICAN

"A wonderful bird is the pelican,
His bill will hold more than his belican.
He can take in his beak
Food enough for a week,
But I'm [darned] if I see how the..."

You see him standing, on the post of a pier.
A bird of dusky color and prodigious size,
with white head and neck during nonbreeding,
more dramatic coloring when rejuvenation is in the air.
His eyes, ringed with orange.
His great throat-pouch flat, pending deployment.

When he travels, he flies in orderly line
with other brown pelicans.
Okay, form up guys!
Heads, hunched back on shoulders!
Bills, resting on breast!

There is a leader, who sets the pattern.
The pattern seems to be this:

Flap, flap, flap, flap. Glide. Flap, flap, flap, flap. Glide.

And so on.

The line flies low, skimming the water.
Again, the line flies high.
Sometimes it undulates, which is highly pleasing.

When a brown pelican is fishing, and he sees a fish,
he twists into a power-dive,
smacking into the water with no regard at all for grace,
just efficiency.

When a pelican decides to take a break from fishing,
he folds his wings and floats buoyantly.
From the shore I saw several dozen, far out at sea.
They looked like the Spanish Armada.

One final curiosity about the pelican.
Although he is obnoxiously noisy in the nest,
when he grows up he takes a vow of silence.
The adult pelican has nothing at all to say,
other than an occasional grunt.
Kind of like some people I know,
before they get their breakfast.

51

SNOWY EGRET

Those that seek Me early shall find Me.
Riches and honor are with Me;
yea, durable riches and righteousness.

Proverbs 8:17-18

Florida, Gulf side, 6:15 a.m. Desire drew me early to the white-sugar sands, for a stab at riches. To my consternation, a man was already headed in from the beach, his plastic bag drooping from the weight. Destination: the shell-washing station. What treasure he beat me to can only be imagined. My eyes narrowed. We didn't speak.

Still, I found a few pretty specimens of my own. My favorite was a rose-speckled scallop, with four golden sunbeams.

At 5:45 the next morning, aflame with determination, I was on the beach.

I had beat the man to the sugar sand.

Alas, it was still "slap dark." Too dark to see the shells.

So I strolled the white rim of the sea, enjoying the sound of the surf.

Suddenly I noticed a Presence walking beside me, just matching my measured pace. She was a snowy egret, *Egretta thula*, engaged in a predawn search of her own.

("She rises also while it is still night, and gives food to her household ....")

How lovely she was, how small and slender, how white against the dark sea. How elegant her lacy plumes, her long black legs, her suave yellow shoes. Bright feet, stepping along in the shallows. Neck tightly coiled, prepared to strike. A dart, a shake of sea spray as she swallowed.

The sky lightened; two gazes met.

At my unveiled proximity, she took to the air. Forty-one-inch span, so they say. But who can measure snow on the wing? Thirteen ounces, so they say. But so much more, to me. I was the richer, for rising early.

And I did get some cool shells.

52

LIVE OAK

Some years ago, I took an art class.
To illustrate the concept of negative space,
the instructor put her hand on her hip.
"If you wanted to draw me in this position," she said,
"your eye would naturally go to my shoulder,
my arm,
my elbow extended,
my hand resting on my hip.
That would be your reality. And you would try to draw that.
But first, I invite you to look at something else.
Look at the shape of the space between my arm and my body.
It may look like nothing. But that space is very important.
Learn to see it, handle it well,
and you will have really learned something."

I was impressed.
Space, as more than emptiness.

A few weeks ago, a tree had to come out of our back yard.
Now, your first thought is probably, "Oh, that's too bad.
Trees are good." I thought the same thing.
I was prepared to be quite sad.

The tree was a live oak, of solid character.
Big and sturdy, it had survived many a storm.
It gave great shade.
It was a bird shelter, a highway for squirrels.

But the tree was in the wrong place.
With every year the wrongness grew more evident.

We have a long, narrow back yard.
Not much room between the house and the fence,
behind which stand utility poles.
In this confined space, without thinking ahead,
someone had planted an oak tree.
The oak tree did what oak trees do.
It grew tall. It flung out its arms.
It ate up the light.
It hogged every dirt nutrient in that part of the yard,
* so the shrubs below it grew sickly.*
It muscled its way into power line territory,
had to be notched.
Fortunately, this periodic breach of the tree's integrity
was on the side away from our house,
so we didn't have to see it.
But the house side of the tree created other problems.
Year by year, below ground,
roots muscled their way under the foundation.
Above, limbs lay heavy on the house, mildewing the roof.
Leaves clogged the gutters.
And still we thought, I suppose,
"Trees are good. Trees are pretty.
Sandy the cat learned to climb in this tree,
and so did our little boys.
Let's not think about it today."

Well, the time finally came to face the music of the chainsaw.
So we hired a tree expert.
A couple of days, and it was over.
The chainsaw was gone, the stump grinder was gone,
a hefty chunk of our bank account was gone.
And so was the tree.

Oh, the emptiness. Woe is me!
But I had not reckoned with the surprising power
of negative space.

How can I describe it to you?
That tree had been pushing space further and further out.
Now, the space came together.
It flowed into the vacuum, created a new reality,
one you can almost touch.
A flooding of our back yard
with the most exquisite golden light.
Gorgeous blue sky, set free.
Beyond the back fence…other beautiful trees!
Trees we can enjoy without the duties of ownership.

Room to breathe. And so, we began to breathe.
The power lines breathed.
The foundation breathed.
The roof breathed.
The grass and shrubs breathed.
I walk out there every morning, just to breathe.

Birds come to inspect the site.
Rusty the dog rolls with great pleasure in the fresh dirt.

As my dad used to say, "Mighty big country!"

53

CHINESE ELM

She has that certain something. Regarding her unusual beauty, people attuned to such things ask me what she is, where they can get one like her. Centerpiece of our small back yard, she's a Chinese elm, thirty-five years old, arms outflung in wide embrace, to the fullness of her height.

Springtime drops over those arms a shimmering frock of palest green, by which she captures hearts as surely as any Southern belle.

In summer her greenery darkens. Her trunk and branches swell with vitality, flinging off gray curls of bark to reveal mahogany smoothness beneath.

In the fall she sets seeds; they fly from her hands on brown-paper wings.

In winter she composes herself to rest. Her poise is a dancer's, balanced, strong, her inclined stillness enlivened by a supple turn where she widens to meet the earth. A bonsai master could not have posed her more charmingly.

But it was Hurricane Bonnie, not bonsai, who shaped her when she was young, the storm twisting, then laying her flat. With hope, and help from neighbors, we hoisted her heaviness upright as best we could, staked her—and somehow she lived. Subsequent years brought more challenges—ice storm, Hurricane Rita, Hurricane Ike, yellow-bellied sapsuckers, severe prunings on her south side to render room for power lines. But in spite of all, this lady-tree grows more beautiful every year. Her life lifts my heart.

She's noted for her hospitality. Little boys enjoyed her shade; so did their dog, of blessed memory. In her branches, birds of every hue and feather—tiny wrens, fierce hawks—have sheltered, sung choruses, mated, or merely paused to catch their breath. You hear a northern cardinal? Look up. There he is, at her crown! Squirrels travel the highway of her arms.

Yesterday I saw a curious sight: In the hot afternoon a squirrel was napping on one branch, smack in the middle of the highway, as if in his scampering he simply gave out—this far and no further. Maybe that droning cicada-music got to him. Who knows? Anyway, there he lay, spraddled on his stomach, chin on Mother Elm's smooth skin, all four legs hanging down, tail stretched out behind. "Surely I have composed and quieted my soul; like a weaned child rests against his mother..." After a time he sprang up and resumed his travels.

In Hebrew imagery, that which lifts the heart, reinvigorates, restores high spirits, is called a Tree of Life. According to Proverbs, Wisdom is a tree of life to those who take hold of her, and happy are those who hold her fast. Her ways are pleasant ways, and all her paths are peace. What do you think? Can one's back yard contain Wisdom—an invitation to prayer, to the perfect stillness of divine embrace? I believe so.

54

Chinese Elm, Revisited

I must write again of my Chinese elm, she who graces our backyard, she whose life lifts my heart. I write in distress, because the Entergy-contracted tree people have come, again. This time they gave her a pruning like none before.

I know it has to be done, for the good of all us grateful consumers of electricity. But this time was drastic. And nothing, really, to be said to the crew. They have their orders.

So I just stood there, in mute agony, enduring the mutilation of my tree. The sound of her arms being fed into the chipper beyond the fence was hard to bear.

From her broad side she still presents a cheerful if thin-lipped façade. But walk ninety degrees around her and your heart will sink, for she is a mere shell of her former being.

My beautiful, stricken tree. In spite of her proven resilience to prunings, ice storms, hurricanes, and sapsuckers, I'm a little uneasy about her health.

So it was that next time my yard chores took me to her vicinity, I put down my tools, and I put my cheek against her bark, and I held her. How silly. But how warm I found her, how fragrant, how solid, how full of life. I had thought to offer comfort. It was she who comforted me.

And lo, she lives on, doing her job: "In the fall she sets seeds; they fly from her hands on brown-paper wings."

Yes, my Chinese elm is obeying Life. She is setting seeds. And plenty of them…

The name "squirrel" floats gently down to us from the Greek *skia*, shadow, and *oura*, tail. Shadow Tail! Family, *Sciuridae*.

It seems the Sciuridae who scurry though our yard have increased in number. I'm used to one or two. Now there are four. At *least* four. From the daily thundering across the roof, it sounds more like a squadron.

This year our Chinese elm has produced a bumper crop of seeds. They must be very delicious. The shadow tails are harvesting them with all their might, gnawing off branch tips, stripping the fruit, then dropping the twiglets on the ground below. It's kind of like consuming fast food and then casually dropping your garbage out the truck window. Or so it seems to me.

Of a morning, of an evening, I see the twiglets raining down. Now and then I go out and rake up the debris. As soon as I go back inside, the twiglets begin to rain down again.

This messiness used to last about a month. After a month, all the seeds were either eaten or wafted away on the wind, and it was over. A month I can tolerate.

But this year, for some unknown reason, we are entering month *three* of the harvest. The perpetual shaking of the tree, the pounds of debris I've raked up, you would not believe.

Arboreal rodents. Shadow tails. They can be annoying. They can also amuse.

Consider the way in which, when the back door opens, they flee for their very lives. They seem to relish the drama. Sometimes they thunder away along the top of the fence.

Other times they barrel down the power line, running one on top, one directly below. Mirror image. I mean, how is that even possible? The shadow tails know…

Consider the time just days ago when one of the little scamps leapt onto the lip of the birdbath for a nice drink.

Only he overshot, and fell in the water.

56

SQUIRREL IN THE STORM

So it came about in a little while,
that the sky grew black with clouds and wind,
and there was a heavy shower.

1 Kings 18:45

After several weeks of intense activity
came a hush,
a quiet time to curl up and read.

It was also the day the drought broke.
And Lord, didn't it rain?

Began with a drizzle,
ramped up to ink-black sky,
settled in for a daylong downpour.
Over and over,
lightning flashed
and thunder boomed.
The trees thrashed about.

I was safe enough in my cozy chair.
I trusted the backyard creatures were safe too,
holed up in burrow and nest.

Around mid afternoon,
perceiving a presence
inconsistent with the dark storm-dance
of the Chinese elm,
I locked up from my reading.

Perched eerily on a branch, a lumpish figure,
with something in its hands.
It turned out to be a squirrel.
Haloed by lightning, unruffled by rain,
unfazed by darkness,
steady in the tumult of the wind,
he was eating Chinese elm seeds.
Dropping branch-tips nonchalantly
onto the ground
for me to rake up later.

Well, one does have to eat.

57

BROTHER, CAN YOU SPARE A CONE?

*Be kindly affectioned toward one another
with brotherly love.*

Romans 12:10

I don't see why they run from me. Perhaps they've heard I spring from a father whose aim was true and whose antipathy toward their race was legend. Whatever the reason, they are a skittish folk, the squirrels, and the minute they spot me at the window or heaven forbid emerging from the house into their back yard, they scatter, as if the forces of Hades were after them.

The other day, on entering their realm from the garage, I nearly dropped my bag of groceries for laughing at their frantic escape—one thundered the entire length of the top rail of the back fence, never faltering, prize secure in his jaws.

Ah, the prize! Perhaps he thought I wanted his September harvest. September is when the magnolia cones begin to ripen.

Magnolia: The very name evokes Southern charm. Creamy white petals, spicy lemon scent, glossy green leaves. After the petals have dropped away, the flower center remains. It matures into a velvety brown cone, from which in the fullness of time emerge plump shiny seeds, of rich Chinese red.

Evidently the seeds are tasty. I've seen mockingbirds dining on them. The squirrels are mad for them. At present, gnawed cones litter the yard. A constellation of dropped seeds gleams 'neath the water in the birdbath.

I do not covet the squirrels' September harvest. I have plenty else to eat. Truly, I come in peace.

My friend Bill Lee loved people. He also loved his little back yard friends, the birds and squirrels.

When Bill died, I was very sad. At the same time, I wanted to express my joy at having known him. So, I bought a clear-tube birdfeeder with six perches, and hung it in the Chinese elm. Behold, the Bill Lee Memorial Birdfeeder.

I didn't want the squirrels emptying the birdfeeder. Which, they will. So I bought a "baffle," a clear dome of rigid plastic. For five years it has done its job. Perfectly. Plus it provides occasional amusement:

Now and then a new squirrel will show up in the yard. I know he's new because he tests the baffle. After studying the matter, and against all advice from his colleagues, he scampers up the tree, out onto the limb, holds on with his back feet while he lowers his front paws down the chain to the top of the dome. From there he ooches down the dome on his belly as far as he can, holding the chain with his back feet. Then, in an act of faith, he lets go. His hope I suppose is to do some kind of acrobatic flip from the rim of the dome to the feeder. But, he cannot. He simply cannot. He has met his limit.

The best part is when he hits the ground and jumps up all nonchalant, like he meant that to happen. One can see the experienced squirrels sniggering at him behind their paws.

Oh well, when I fill the feeder I manage to "spill" enough on the ground to keep everyone happy.

This early morning there were the usual small birds on the feeder, and the usual large birds foraging in the grass below. And, bounding or belly-creeping about, the usual gray squirrels.

By his configuration, small size, and tentative manner, I took one squirrel to be a male trainee. He scampered up the tree, made his way out the branch from which the feeder hangs. Moving past the feeder, he turned and regarded it. He seemed to be applying some critical thinking to the situation. Evidently he's been told or experienced for himself that it's futile to shimmy down the feeder-chain, for once one reaches the baffle and attempts to ease down its dome to the feeder, one is sure to be cast embarrassingly to the ground.

Still, one is hungry. Conventional wisdom would direct the trainee to scamper back down the tree and reach the freely available ground-seeds that way. But it seems he had an idea for a shortcut. He could simply drop from branch to ground. A mere six feet. The drop would be his own choice. Not something imposed on him.

He gathered his courage, made several feints at taking the plunge, only to draw back. He seemed to be wracked with indecision. Finally it was all just too much; he lay down on his stomach on the branch, with his little paws hanging down.

Of course from the other side of the window I was gleefully exhorting him to get up again. On your feet, Son of Squirrel! You can do it!

Just as I was about to give up on him, he got up. He rose, assumed the pose, and dropped.

He almost landed on a white-wing dove. Which would have been pretty funny, at least to me.

Squirrel Enchantress

Today, the backyard is empty of entertainment, save for the droning of the cicadas.

But now comes a squirrel. She scampers past the birdfeeder, out to a slight fork in the branch of the Chinese elm, where she stops.

Now, this you should know about that slight fork. It's an observation station, where various creatures post themselves to stare into the house.

("Is the coast is clear? Or is the Great Human at her alarming exercise, just inside the glass? I mean, it looks as if she's running toward us! Yet, she never gets anywhere. Still, one cannot be too careful.")

At nesting time, our male northern cardinal perches at this fork, to give me warning looks. Our alpha blue jay perches there to tell me he'd like to bathe in the birdbath but will not, as long as he can see me. Et cetera.

So today it's a lady squirrel who stations herself there. The sight of me at my exercise must make her tired; after looking me over, she drapes herself across the branch, as if for a little rest.

Gazing toward me, her black eyes give away nothing. Her belly supported by the branch, tail hanging down behind, she drops her arms down in front, daintily crosses her wrists, then grasps one paw with the other, palm to palm.

Stop here, dear reader, and try that pose for yourself! She must practice squirrel ballet, or rodent yoga—where else would she have learned it?

So she regards me calmly for, oh, five minutes.

Then she arises from her rest, drops semi-gracefully to the ground below, and commences to root in the grass for sunflower seeds.

She finds one, lifts it toward me, paws in prayer position. We exchange a heartfelt reverence: Namaste.

Which almost causes me to fall off the elliptical laughing…

HOLY KISS

As I write it's 38.7°F outside, and raining. I see a sodden, shivering, string-tailed squirrel 'neath the birdfeeder, foraging for seeds. Poor thing. We're all in the iron grip of winter, and spring will never come.

Ah, but the white-winged doves have been giving each other the glad eye, murmuring throatily, "Who cooks for you?"

The red-shouldered hawks have hushed their calling, which means the work of nest-building is underway.

The mockingbirds are mobilizing for the Dance.

Here's a valentine for you, a very old one, tucked in the Hebrew scriptures:

The Song of Songs, which is Solomon's:
May he kiss me with the kisses of his mouth!

The book of Genesis reports that Adam was brought into being by the mouth of Adonai. Life begins by *mitat neshikah*, a Divine Kiss.

And how does life end? At the close of Deuteronomy, Moses dies *al pi Adonai*. By the mouth of Adonai. Jewish commentators have taken this literally: God drew Moshe home with a kiss.

Back to Song of Solomon, a book worth reading: "Arise, my darling, my beautiful one, and come along. For behold, the winter is past, the rain is over and gone. The flowers have already appeared in the land; the time has arrived for pruning the vines, and the voice of the turtledove has been heard in our land. The fig tree has ripened its figs, and the vines in blossom have given forth their fragrance. Arise, my darling, my beautiful one, and come along!"

The kiss of spring is coming. Believe it!

COCKATIEL

When our boys were young, we acquired a cockatiel, one of those elegant-looking birds with dark gray feathers, bright yellow head, orange cheeks, and dashing crest.

We did not buy him. He simply showed up, one glorious summer day. Dave and Robert ran inside to tell me. By the time I got outside, news of the exotic visitor had spread. Neighbors had gathered, as neighbors will.

The cockatiel was perched perhaps ten feet up, in a tree. Encouraged by the crowd, Dave shimmied up the tree to try to catch him.

The moment of capture was the first and only time I've heard Dave swear. It was a shock to know that my child had such a creative vocabulary at the tender age of seven. And now, our whole side of the street knew it.

On the other hand, who could blame him? For the cockatiel did not suffer capture in a baseball cap quietly. He took his ounce of flesh.

The bird went unclaimed. (I wonder why!) After a few days, we decided he was ours.

Because of his feisty nature, we named him Spike. He was a spirited little fellow, with a personality to match his vivid coloring. And what an entertainer! He could sing and dance. He had star quality.

Tasha the cat, for one, couldn't take her eyes off him. In fact, her attention would get so intense that we would have to speak to her sharply. At that, she would stalk away, with a twitch of her coat, a lash of her tail. Tasha the Huntress, thwarted.

One thing about Spike I particularly remember is that he liked to start his day early. His cage was on the sun porch: skylights above, kitchen window to the east. The moment he perceived that night was retreating in favor of dawn, Spike would snap to attention. Sleep would drop from him instantly. He would burst forth into rollicking, piercing, window-rattling song. His joy knew no bounds. Notes poured forth, a relentless stream from his light-filled little breast.

Raise a shout for the Lord, all the earth!
Come into His presence with shouts of joy!

The only problem was that it was still dark, and the people of Spike's house were not quite ready to fling their hearts open to the new day. They preferred to rest and reflect until the sun had officially risen.

So we learned to cover Spike's cage with a blanket at bedtime. He was content to have it so. He did not reproach us, but waited quietly for our version of the dawn, which he would still meet with shouts of joy, whenever it came.

We have a cat at our house, Sandy by name. She turns thirteen this month, a venerable age for a cat. This is a birthday tribute to her. This is the story of how she's encountered various trials, and still managed to live long and prosper. There is in our house a certain young man, our younger son. Home from college after some weeks away, he noticed that Sandy is walking rather stiffly these days, that she has an even grumpier attitude than he remembered. So he asked her, with the presumption of youth, "Sandy, why are you such a Gloomy Old Hag?"

Poor Sandy. As if she hasn't enough to deal with, now she has a new name. For I'm afraid it stuck. Even with me, her closest ally, because I happen to think Gloomy Old Hag has a certain style about it.

Yes, Sandy has to put up with a lot. Another male of the household likes to play with Sandy. As you may know, cats are not real big on games. Nevertheless, for thirteen years he has enjoyed playing patty cake with Sandy, wherein he holds her in his lap and claps her front paws together while reciting the time-honored rhyme. His little boys, now grown, used to love this! He's sure that Sandy loves it, too. If so, she hides it well. Her eyes dilate menacingly, she lays her ears back…and she endures. She keeps her temper, knowing that when he puts her down, at least she'll have the satisfaction of stalking away with dramatic tail lashes.

Another game he likes to play with Sandy is "Tonto and the Lone Ranger." This is his patented invention. Feel free to use it if there's a cat at your house. Just make sure your Kitty has been declawed. To play this fun game, you are the Lone Ranger. Kitty is Tonto. You capture Tonto. As she struggles to get free, she will likely start to voice her displeasure. This is your cue. As she meows, just cup your hand over her mouth and make a quick succession of taps. This will produce a reasonable facsimile of Tonto's Indian war cry. This effect is guaranteed to produce great hilarity for the Lone Ranger, and more dramatic tail lashing opportunities for Tonto.

The Lone Ranger also persecutes Sandy by accusing her of being genetically defective. The evidence he cites is that unlike her predecessor Tasha the Mighty Huntress, Sandy has never displayed the slightest inclination to hunt birds. To her credit, Sandy accepts this slander with supreme indifference. She knows who she is, thank you very much, and if she prefers a nonviolent path, what of it? Further, unlike Tasha, who died at two, Sandy has managed to live thirteen years, which blows the genetically defective theory neatly out of the water.

Poor Gloomy Old Hag. To add to the burden she carries, she continues to have to endure her younger brother the dog. Since Rusty joined us, she's worked with him, trying to teach him dignity and restraint. She has repeatedly modeled for him how one polite creature greets another. Her modeling method? When she finds him in a quiet and teachable mood, in other words asleep, she approaches him calmly and touches noses. But Rusty just doesn't get it. More often than not, he leaps up eagerly, returns her greeting with lots of undignified sniffing about her person. He still doesn't realize this is not the way to bond with a cat.

Then there's my part in Sandy's travails. I admit I'm guilty. Knowing as I do that middle-aged ladies of every species must undergo certain dietary adjustments if they want to keep their girlish figures, I've reduced Sandy's food ration a bit. But Sandy is not interested in keeping her girlish figure. She wants food. And so by morning she's pretty desperate. Though I will note in my defense that she is far from wasting away.

A further thing I do to her, once a year, is stuff her into a cat carrier and take her to the vet. As if the mortifying examination and painful shots are not enough, invariably the good doctor notices the black marks on her face.(She's a yellow tabby, but her mom was a calico.) He always says, "Look, ha, ha, she must have gotten into the black grease!" Sandy is not amused. Not when she was a kitten, not now, not ever.

Here's one more tribulation worth mentioning: Even after thirteen years with us, she still doesn't understand about showers. Human showering worries her greatly. Any use of water other than for drinking is, to her, a horrible thought. (I think that's why she makes a food sacrifice every morning, placing one precious star of her Little Friskies into her water bowl as a propitiation to the water gods.) Anyway, if she happens to become aware that one of her humans is showering, she takes up her post nearby and meows anxiously until the human emerges and she can see that all is well. Then, in grateful relief, she winds about the human's legs, in the process bestowing golden fur, which is awfully hard to remove from wet skin.

I love my Gloomy Old Hag, and I salute her on her birthday.

Well, Sandy made it sixteen years. She would be the last to want a sappy send-off. Not cat-like. So we held her Holy Saturday funeral in silence. Her younger brother the dog lay down by her grave and moaned, but other than that, no words were spoken.

She had fallen silent herself the day before—she chose Good Friday to stop her awful railing against blindness, to stop walking in pitiful frustrated circles.

As the day unfolded, she stopped all extraneous movement and sound altogether. The bottom line for her was to settle against my heart, purring, and wait. Enough for her to be in my arms, to know that Austin, Robert, and Rusty the dog were close by, keeping watch.

And so Easter weekend was especially poignant this year. I confess I am taking the death of this faithful little feline very hard. But I make no excuses. She was dear, and sixteen years of friendship is a long time.

This morning as I dressed to go to Bible study, I heard something outside, a voice close to Sandy's resting place. It was a male northern cardinal, singing his heart out, no doubt to attract a lovely lady of his species. But I took it as a note of encouragement, a suggestion to give thanks, remember, and let Sandy go.

The message? "What? Cheer! What? Cheer! What? Cheer!" There are friends gathering, a Bible lesson to be taught. So one had best take heart, and get on with it.

So it goes, in the life of a family, the life of a community, the life of a church. There will continue to be long stretches of "ordinary time," punctuated by surging joy, and body-blows of pain. Through it all, we keep loving, trusting, and praying, often with sighs too deep for words. We keep claiming the anguish of Good

Friday, the hush of Holy Saturday, the glory and power and promise of Easter.

And underneath it all, the everlasting arms.

Deuteronomy 33:27

LIZARD ON A LEAF WITH DIAMONDS

It was early morning, cool for August. As the sun rose, I sat on the patio, near a border I had planted—big blue liriopes, pineapple sage, and a split-leaf philodendron—one I had rescued from pot-bound neglect.

Sun warming my face, I was reading a new translation of Psalm 104:

How many are the things you have made, O Lord; you have made them all with wisdom; the earth is full of your creations … All of them look to you to give them their food when it is due. Give it to them, they gather it up; open your hand, they are well satisfied; hide your face, they are terrified; take away their breath, they perish and turn again into dust; send back your breath, they are created, and you renew the face of the earth.

I looked at the plants and thought of their roots thrust deep in the dark earth, drawing up what they need to live. The philodendron in particular caught my eye. It's a recovering plant, rewarding me these days with an energetic display of broad green leaves. I noticed that its leaves were spangled with dewdrops. The leaves are green meadows, with shimmering diamonds strewn about.

While lost in this reverie, I heard a rustling, and there came forth a green lizard. He was a young lizard, graceful and sure-footed. He had a little round belly, and a narrow chest under which lay tiny ribs. I could see him breathing. He cast his dark eye my way—I was only a couple of feet from him.

I guess he decided I was okay, for he ventured out onto the sunlit meadow. He approached the first diamond. Out came the tip of a pink tongue, and he lapped it up. He drank several more diamonds, then he was gone, though I could still hear him moving about in the shade of the pineapple sage. In a little while he reappeared, dashing out to grab a small insect.

By this time I had seen others of his tribe beginning their day—a great big daddy lizard, and a tiny brown hatchling. They all seemed well satisfied. Daily bread, earth renewed—what more could they want?

The green lizards bore a bumper crop this year. Adults, intermediates, miniatures—a thriving community. I see them, stealth-hunting at dawn. At high noon, a small Jehu or two, skittering across the patio. (II Kings: "It looks like the driving of Jehu son of Nimshi, for he drives like a maniac.")

Now and then, at evensong, I see one stretched lengthwise on a liriope leaf. Fragile grace, so neatly arranged for sleep. It's okay to love them, so long as I don't touch.

However, if I catch one in the house, I stroke his little head before I put him outside. At my touch, he closes his eyes. Whether in resignation, pleasure, or plotting how best to rend me with his tiny teeth, who knows? Whatever his thoughts may be, 'tis grace enough for me, to hold his life in my hands.

One creature I want to touch but never shall is the swallow-tail kite. I saw him yesterday, soaring high above Phelan Boulevard. I know his flight now, no need for the forked tail to give him away. Oh the grace of this falcon-like hunter. The size, the strength of him, arms outstretched. The tuxedoed elegance, the lightness of him—he pulls me, with cords of love.

But consider the curve of his claws, the surgeon beak. Even should he condescend to stand before me, heart may touch him, but hands dare not.

Once a beautiful hazard named Maxine the barred owl allowed me to caress the place where her wing should be. We had a significant moment, we brown-eyed girls. I in my dangerous humanness, she is her stunning silk dress, one arm pinned.

As to close encounters with raptors, that will have to do for me. Except for my imagination, which is not constrained....

Flight patterns: Have you noticed how the bright northern cardinal dips when he flies—a garland of smiles? Smiles he gives, and color. But the crimson is wild. Should he allow a human to hold him, which assuredly he will not—if he can help it—be mindful of that seed-crushing beak, lest thy finger take on his hue!

67

Strength in Numbers

In our massive wild pear tree, a cacophony of blue jays, hastily assembled to give what-for to an Intruder, not positively ID'd but believed to be a falcon.

Beneath the birdfeeder, foraging for sunflower seeds, a covey of white-wing doves. I notice some have pale blue orbital rings around their eyes, and some don't. Bird book reveals it's a matter of maturity—the juvies will eventually earn their blue.

Flitting about their daily rounds, a family of northern cardinals—mom, dad, two adolescents learning the ropes.

Seen in airspace above:

Snow-plumed escadrille of egrets, lit by the morning sun, heads tucked back on shoulders, legs trailing behind, winging their way to work. Silent save for one, who utters a low, hoarse grunt.

Seen in Hardin County:

Circling just above our small lake at Beech Creek, a golden eagle. This sighting via a phone consult, in which the excited witness (my sister) feeds me details as I research the emerging picture on the Internet and in the bird book. Who knew that golden eagles are occasional stragglers to these parts? We decide, sympathetically if unscientifically, that his laryngitic yelping must be an attempt to locate his fellows.

68

Look Alive!

Oh, how I cherish the ever-emerging poem of my back yard. Each season brings joy. Right now it's the spring-green of Chinese elm, snow-white of wild pear (flurries and drifts in the driveway—as leaves arrive, the petals are going), the splash of azaleas, the careening of those small charioteers the lizards, and of course, the lively singing of the birds.

Evidently they've heard of John Wesley, who exhorts us to "sing lustily and with good courage. Beware of singing as if you were half dead, or half asleep; but lift up your voice with strength."

Lift up your voice! Look alive!

69

A HOST OF BUTTERFLIES

In a flower bed, at the foot of a crape myrtle, stands a shrub with an interesting name: *Duranta repens*. Sky-flower. This dazzling creature is dressed, at the moment, in rich green. And she is graced with masses of the most exquisite flowers—deep purple, edged in white. The brightness of her beauty draws me close.

I'm not the only one.

As I approach, what should I see on *Duranta* but a host of butterflies. Five monarchs, regal in orange and black, wings opening and closing in ecstasy. Two clouded sulphurs, radiant in yellow. And several small, unidentified *Lepidoptera*: brown, with touches of red.

How close can I get without disturbing them? Soon I'm practically standing in *Duranta*. All around me the exuberant nectar-feasting continues. I can hear the rustle of their wings. Well, this is almost too much joy.

Feeling I've trespassed on holy ground, I step back onto the grass, from whence I continue to drink in this gorgeous picture, all the cares and concerns in my heart and mind warmed and softened under God's good sunshine.

Yes, it's almost too much miracle. So I retreat another step.

O, Love that will not let me go ...

Two of the monarchs detach from the feast, flutter to me, spiral down my body and back up again, brushing my skin and my clothes with their wings.

Maybe it's my Black Orchid perfume. Maybe they think I'm a flower. I don't know. But I feel loved. Deeply loved. As if I'm a cherished part of an unfolding plan...

Have you ever innocently opened your front door, and there on the welcome mat is a creature so gorgeous it takes your breath away? Happened to me Monday. Sadly for the creature, it was dead. But it looked alive, ready to resume its "leaping greenly."

It was a member of the family *Tettigoniidae*, otherwise known as katydids. Or in British-speak, bush crickets. Mine (for I've kept it) is a heavenly shade of emerald green. A compact, perky little being, even in death, with its neatly composed limbs, flat face cocked alertly to one side, bright brown eyes that seem to see something I cannot.

But its glory is its wings. The wings, you see, are leaves. Shape, texture, veining, color... How can a wing be a leaf? You'll have to trust me.

A holy hush; now comes Wednesday afternoon. I am on the back patio, watering the parched lantanas. Oblivious to the caressing breeze and the sunny blue above, I am feeling a little low. Why so cast down, my soul? Who knows? I move through the duty of watering. Discipline, yes.

A butterfly joins me. Charming monarch, she floats about, investigating the roses, sipping lantana nectar, dodging spray from the hose. I suspect what might be about to happen, for it's happened to me before. Sure enough, after a few more rounds of our dance, she flies directly to me, and brushes my cheek.

This should be grace enough for one girl for one week. But the story isn't over, for I have left the back door open...

Later, at the kitchen sink, I catch a movement on the counter. Green lizard. He dives for cover. He's fast, but I'm faster. Having seized lizards before, I know I have this one in an awkward place: I'm gripping his vulnerable little belly. Afraid to hurt him, trying to work out how to transfer my grip to the safe area behind his jaws, I am flustered. If he gets away, he'll be gone, and a few days later I'll find a desiccated little corpse in the corner. What to do?

He knows what to do. As I gingerly pin him against the counter by his tender middle, he whips around and seizes my finger in his mouth. I burst out laughing. Now HE has ME, with all the fury of his little being. Which unplanned turn of the dramatic universe allows me to refine my grip and carry him outside. As soon as his feet feel the ground, and I tell him it's okay to go, he releases my finger and goes.

71

GIANT SWALLOWTAIL

I came home from a morning of Grand Jury so awful that I had to lie down for a while. In fact, my husband told me that my face was gray.

After a time I got up, still fatigued, still pondering the horror of what people are capable of doing to each other. As I walked through the sunporch on my way to the kitchen for a cup of tea, bright wings outside the glass caught my eye. *Papilio cresphontes*, giant swallowtail. How did I know her? Not for nothing did my brother and I work so hard as children, with homemade nets and butterfly book!

Giant swallowtails fly high and fast, are seldom seen, and when seen, are exceedingly difficult to capture. Evidently this one intended to capture me. As if looking over her shoulder to make sure I noticed, she lit on a branch of glossy green jasmine, and casually spread her wings.

By this pose she was breaking an important butterfly rule: At rest, your wings are to be folded neatly together, over your back.

I darted for my camera. When I returned, she had not moved. In spite of my fear that she would bolt, I opened the door, and crept onto the patio. She allowed it. Deciding to risk everything, I moved closer. Again, she allowed it. Soon I was practically on her.

Unmoving, she held her ground. Head up, antennae alert, wings still spread. First I photographed her back: dark body, ebony wings, with intersecting lines of yellow spots. On the inner edges of her hind wings, two crossed "eyes"—bright orange, with blue eyebrows. Ah, a comedienne!

I moved around to her other side. Regally upright she remained. Radiant undercarriage: What a contrast to her dark back. Body and wings, bright buttery yellow. As the old song says, "You make my sad heart jump for joy." That, she did!

Her nectar-sipping proboscis was tightly curled, as if in contemplation, and the dark domes of her eyes regarded me. Several more photographs this beauty allowed me. Then she was gone.

Later that afternoon a friend called. As she shared the mixed emotions she was feeling over the imminent marriage of her eldest son—the joy of his taking a bride, the grief of her little boy never being her little boy again—I wandered around the backyard, cell phone to my ear, listening. Finding myself in the myrtle grove amidst the roses, I paused to pluck a couple of spent blooms. Behold, something touched my cheek. It was she again. Giant swallowtail. *Papilio cresphontes.* Brushing by to say…what?

72

POSSUM

Cold day, high noon.

And I on my sun porch with book on my lap had just settled my brain for a nice ham sandwich, when out on the lawn there appeared a dread Omen…

What is it?

Off with my readers, and on with the other—O send for the infantry, send for my mother! For what to my horror is now in play, but a hideous possum, headed my way.

Now, possums are creepy enough when you see them at night. You know, that ghoulish thing they have going on: ghastly pale fur, spectral skull, glittering eyes…

But this was worse, and here's why. Possums are supposed to be nocturnal. So, clearly, this one ambling toward me in broad daylight must be rabid.

Rabies! Great Jumping Jehoshaphat! Never mind there's glass between us. I scream like a ninny, as if the possum were leaping even now to latch foaming jaws onto my throat.

And then, and then, it was interesting how quickly I moved from terror to violence. Not because I love violence, oh no, but because at certain times, it's my duty to act.

And now I imagine myself Atticus Finch, stepping into the street to protect all I hold dear, raising my rifle to the shambling snapping sickness that used to be a dog. Or in this case, a possum. Shall I suffer a daytime possum to live? No.

Fortunately for the possum, fortunately for the side of the garage, I had no weapon close to hand, and no real desire to use one even if I had. Fortunately for all, something shifted in me from a vehement "no" about that possum to a measured "maybe."

As I observed him more closely, more impartially, the storm in me abated. It dawned on me that he seemed perfectly well. In fact, he was simply easing along through the azaleas, searching I suppose for something to eat.

Evidently finding nothing of interest, he turned on his heel, or should I say heels, and went back as he came, in good order, through the gate.

I wanted to know more. Research revealed that possums are very unlikely to carry rabies. In fact, they're more or less impervious to rabies.

Even so, they're easily frightened. For possums, playing possum is no subterfuge. On the contrary, when they're scared, they faint dead away. In all sincerity, their gums drop back from their teeth, they emit a smell like death, and it takes a good while for them to come around again.

Bless their hearts.

Possums are hardworking, diligent parents. One reason you may see a possum in daylight is that it was too cold the night before for him to hunt. And now, he's hungry.

He and his family are hungry.

73

BIG THICKET

Mysterious, magical, tucked away, teeming with life. Thus did the young man describe the Big Thicket.

His photographs were exquisite, his comments simple and soft spoken, from a heart full for his subject.

He's helping with a Thicket species inventory.

With 300 kinds of birds, 1,000 kinds of flowers, myriad mushrooms, shiploads of salamanders, loads of lichens, swarms of snakes (ewww), tons of turtles, streams of slime molds, floods of fungi—well, you get the idea—there's plenty to count.

He named large creatures: bobcats, black bears, panthers, wolves. But his particular eye, trained first in fine art and now biology, is for the small things.

He was chasing a frog, which hopped in a log, in whose interior he found: bouquets of glowing pearls! Tiny fungi they were, stunning beauty hidden, till the accident of his intrusion, the skilful reverent application of his camera.

He described the Thicket as a tranquil place with lurking dangers: quicksand. Coral snakes. Gators. Stinging things. Spider webs in your face, when you're intent on the leaf litter at your feet. Snapping turtles, with jaws to take off a toe. Several kinds of hideous leeches (Get them off me, Rosie!)

He described one incident in which he'd been on the ground for hours, trying for the perfect photographic rendering of some small growing thing. Turning to pack up his gear, he beheld a face, regarding him. It was a copperhead snake, motionless, inscrutable, well within striking distance. He wondered whether to attempt a mighty spring out of range, or take its picture. He took its picture. A portrait I'll not soon forget. That chalk-pale skin! Those cold eyes! Those non-lips!

The team doing the inventory have found species not seen for years, and others new to science. Evidently all you have to do is scoop up a net-full of slimy leaf debris, spread it out, and look. In that net-full could be 100 kinds of critters. One new species they've found is an insect, member of the "water boatman" tribe. Did you know that one may stealthily slip a microphone into the swamp and hear plenty? Did you know that one water boatman species is said to produce more sound-power relative to its body size than any other creature on earth?

Did you know that a lichen (that ruffly stuff that grows on trees) is a strange relationship in which fungi enslave algae? Let my algae go!

Some of the colors he's seen in the Thicket are so rich, so saturated, that there's no way even the most sophisticated camera can do them justice. And then the light changes, the color disappears … I scrawled my notes that night on both sides of a business card, all I had in my purse. And now I offer my findings to you. Joy, joy, joy!

74

On the Ivory Bill

At dawn, I wake to the prospect of adventure. By ten I stand near the Neches River. She who brings joy, she who bears us up in our little boats (and barges, and ships, and water skis…) Ancient stream, never to be cut off.

As we motor forth from Riverfront Park on that fine excursion craft "Ivory Bill," it's easy to see humankind at work: Train lumbering across lift bridge, sounds of clanking machinery emanating from warehouses, diver up briefly from investigating a sunken barge, thunder as we pass under Interstate 10, sheriff's boat whisking by. Industry, enterprise, surveillance, repair.

Leaving this behind, we move northward on the Neches, into another world.

The Big Thicket: water lapping, with low sounds, by the shore. Peace.

Peace. The better to experience swallows on the wing, egrets stabbing fry, anhinga stretched to dry, bulrushes (is that a tiny woven basket, covered with pitch?)

We glide into Ten Mile Creek, which becomes…the Enchanted Woods. (I know this place, this feeling of body slowing, heart quickening…) Water deep, water dark. Tupelo trees, slow-growing cypress with leaves of lacy green, curtains of Spanish moss, strange twisted stumps with mysterious holes and hollows, narrow channels, radiating like spokes of a wheel. Majestic blue heron, undulating ahead of us. Burst of black and white, crested in red: Pileated woodpecker flicks across. Call of northern cardinal, Carolina chickadee, a loud warbler no one presumes to name. Spider lilies, purple iris, arrowroot…

We take a water sample. We learn that baby shrimp are born here, that shrimplets hide "in the grass, in the knees, in the pleats of the trees" until they grow big enough to swim downriver to the Gulf.

We listen to a recording of a folk song about the Belle of the Neches, a dashing steamboat who plied our river in the nineteenth century, carrying cotton and passengers. Her day passed. She sank long ago. But the song concludes with the spine-tingling sound of her resurrected whistle.

There is sadness. There is joy.

I thought there could be no brighter red than a northern cardinal (*Cardinalis cardinalis*.) But then, in a sanctuary near the sea, I saw a scarlet tanager. Those who know describe the red of a male scarlet tanager as "brilliant." The sunlit glory of this one certainly rendered our little knot of birders speechless. And some of them had seen a thing or two.

After an interval my companion and I eased on up the wooded trail to a secluded glade, where we sat on a bench, sharing a juicy orange. A prince of an orange. An orange among oranges.

Across the small clearing, at the edge of the dark woods, was a "drip," a trickle of water coursing down into a small bowl. Within moments a brown thrasher peeked out from the shadows, eying the water. Seeing us, he hastily withdrew. But not before we glimpsed feathers of rich chestnut, the afternoon sun touching them ever so briefly into molten copper. And I, I imagined his eye, of bright gold: Thrasher eyes have flashed at me in my own yard, for the impertinence of coming too near a nest. So I know those eyes...

Another moment and our quiet watching was rewarded by the appearance of a prothonatory warbler, who flirted his lemon yellow up, down, and all around, seeming to relish our admiration.

And then, oh tiny Star, a ruby-throated hummingbird. He commenced such an extended display of hovering up and down the narrow ribbon of water, sipping and splashing, iridescence flashing in the sun, as to gladden the weariest of hearts.

And then, what joy, we found our way to a rookery. Great egrets, snowy egrets, cormorants, anhingas—such a commingled, intertribal gathering of water birds, assembled in crowded order, to get on with the business of raising families. Clustered thick they were, preening, courting, carrying twigs, sitting on nests... Oh the beauty of them. And the noise! The cormorants are pleased to make a grunting sound when roosting. Yes, like pigs! Or perhaps bullfrogs. Which is somewhat unnerving, coming from a bird.

I save for last the stars of the rookery, at least in my eyes. These are the pink bishops, otherwise known as roseate spoonbills. So dashing, these princes of the church. Bright, bright pink, like the rosy fingers of dawn. Wings edged with deep scarlet. Yellow epaulets. And orange tails. Who could have designed such splendid array?

76

THE MONARCH AND THE ROSE

The Bible, sacred library, book of books,
writings of people long ago.
And we, a people yet alive, seeking wisdom.
And so, from time to time
we take from the shelf of the sacred library
a book of wisdom,
perhaps the Song of Songs, by King Solomon the wise.
And if it be the Song to which we open,
from the first line, "O give me the kisses of your mouth"
to the last line "Hurry, my beloved…"
'tis likely to make us catch our breath.
Listen for instance to a holy conversation,
three thousand years old:

The Woman says,

> *Wake up, North Wind,*
> *   get moving, South Wind!*
> *Breathe on my garden,*
> *   fill the air with spice fragrance.*
> *Oh, let my lover enter his garden!*
> *   Yes, let him eat the fine, ripe fruits.*

The Man says,

> *I went to my garden, dear friend, best lover!*
> *   breathed the sweet fragrance.*
> *I ate the fruit and honey,*
> *   I drank the nectar and wine.*

And God says,

    Eat, O friends, drink, and make you merry, O well-beloved.

Autumn 2014, I read that delightful directive,
and I think to myself:

All this breathing, and sweetness, and nectar, and wine:
With such an October, it does come to mind.
The warmth of the sun, the cool of the air,
The blue of the sky, the moon so fair…

Wasn't it remarkable, to be blessed
with such a run
of perfect October days?

I know the cold days are coming:

As they work to stash their harvest,
the squirrels are furring up before my eyes,
luxurious coats of silver gray
and the Chinese elm has set her seeds.

Yes, winter is coming.
But it's not here yet.
October, with all her charms,
and I'm drinking it in.
In my patio garden the wind carries the spice-fragrance
of basil,
scent of rosemary,
of pineapple sage,
crowned at last, as promised, with spires of scarlet,
nodding in the breeze.

Make you merry, O well-beloved…

One day a movement catches my eye.
I look to the knockout roses in the back hedge,
the knockouts, whose flowers flame red in the sun.
On one perfect rose, a monarch butterfly.
And such a monarch.
Of regal size, a monarch of the first degree.
As the rose she drinks from, lit like flame by the sun.
On the ebony edges of her wings, double strand of pearls.

And the prayer wheel of my heart turns,
turns to the Song of Songs:

> *How beautiful you are, my darling.*
> *How beautiful.*
> *Your cheeks are lovely with ornaments,*
> *your neck with strings of beads.*
> *You have made my heart beat faster*
> *with a single glance,*
> *with a single strand of your necklace.*

Thus robed in orange, and ebony, and strands of pearls
the monarch butterfly moves about the rose,
face buried in beauty,
wings folded, mostly.
But every heart-stopping while, she opens her wings
to their full four-inch radiance.
And in the shadow of those wings, we imagine,
the rose sings for joy…

Song of Songs:

> *I am a rose of Sharon, a lily of the valleys.*

My beloved is clear-skinned and ruddy,
preeminent among ten thousand.
His head is finest gold;
his locks are curled, and black as a raven …
His mouth is full of sweetness…
This is my beloved, and this is my friend…

What an interesting book, the Song of Songs,
tucked among the wisdom writings.

Does the Song speak "merely" of King Solomon
and his bride, the Shulamite,
one of his many, many wives and concubines,
perhaps his favorite, and wouldn't we all
like to be the favorite,
the apple of someone's eye?
To hear these words:

> *Every part of you is fair, my darling.*
> *You have captured my heart.*

Captured my heart, yes. Make me a captive, Lord.
Does the Song of Songs speak of the Creator
and his beloved Creation?

In the book of the prophet Isaiah [62:5] we read,

> *As a bridegroom rejoices over his bride,*
> *So will your God rejoice over you.*

In the book of the prophet Zephaniah [3:17],

> *He will rejoice over you and be glad,*
> *he will shout over you*

with jubilation.
He will soothe with his love...

Does the Song speak of all of us, to all of us,
generation after generation, generations not yet born,
of life, of love, of longing and belonging,
of memory, of meaning, of family, of blessing, of hope?
Strange stirrings of the heart,
all the while knowing we are not the first to feel
these things?
Does it speak the language of unexpected encounter,
say, a butterfly on a rose on a perfect October day?

To all the above, we may answer, with gratitude:
Yes. All that.
That is the wisdom of the Song.
That's why it was canonized.
That's why we've kept it.

There's another writing I want to share, because,
like Solomon's Song, it's beautiful, unusual, startling even.
Words by Joseph Swain of Birmingham, England,
engraver's apprentice,
convert to Christianity in the late eighteenth century,
who poured his poetic temperament
and his newly directed feelings
into verses that later became an early American folk-hymn,
set to the lovely and deeply mysterious
Southern shape-note tune Samanthra.

Be the tune as it may, the words spring
directly from the Song of Songs,
spring like living water to help Joseph Swain describe a man,
one Jesus of Nazareth, Immanuel, God among us,

who came that we might have life, and have it more abundantly,
even as we live, as we must, in the valley of the shadow…

As you will imagine when you hear it, Swain's song in its day
must surely have raised the color
in many a youthful and not so youthful cheek,
must have touched hearts of all ages
with its haunting sadness entwined
with its promise of beauty that lives forever.
Beauty that lives forever. Listen to the first stanza, and the last:

> *His voice, as the sound of the dulcimer sweet,*
> *is heard through the shadows of death;*
> *The cedars of Lebanon bow at His feet,*
> *the air is perfumed with His breath.*
> *His lips as the fountain of righteousness flow,*
> *that waters the garden of grace,*
> *From which their salvation the people shall know,*
> *and bask in the smiles of His face…*

> *This is my Belovèd, His form is divine;*
> *His vestments shed odor around;*
> *The locks on His head are as grapes on the vine,*
> *when autumn with plenty is crowned.*
> *The roses of Sharon, the lilies that grow*
> *in the vales, on the banks of the streams*
> *On His cheeks in the beauty of excellence blow;*
> *His eyes are as quivers of beams.*
> *His voice as the sound of the dulcimer sweet*
> *is heard through the shadows of death;*
> *The cedars of Lebanon bow at His feet,*
> *the air is perfumed with His breath.*

Strange language, strangely beautiful.
May it work tonight with the Song of Songs

to quicken our imaginations
to tune our senses to a different frequency
to open us in a new way
to all the dimensions of beauty and excellence around us.
May it remind us that in sunshine and in shadow,
there is Life with us, always, always,
and closer than our breath.
A Life which invites, "Make you merry, O well-beloved."
Amen.

77

Fly Me to the Moon

My eyes spring open in the dark. There's that music again. Music of the Spheres. So early. It would be nice to go back to sleep. Oh well.

Front yard. Five a.m. Bathrobe and binoculars. Look straight up. See that star cloud? That's no cloud, that's the Pleiades, the elegant Seven Sisters. See how the binoculars make them spring to life? And look! There's Orion, the Hunter.

What *is* that crazy music?? It's been playing in human hearts a long, long time.

To the east, our brilliant neighbor Venus, bright Morning Star. Shining rock-steady beside her, her brother-planet, Saturn. Saturn, eight hundred million miles away. I can almost see his rings.

All nature sings, and round me rings...

Have you ever run your finger around the lip of a crystal goblet? To see Saturn is like that. Saturn, surrounded by his crystalline rings and his thirty-one moons. Thirty-one moons. Can you imagine? Heavenly choir, all processing in dignified formation, all singing on key.

Well, all but one.

Who's the eccentric lady with the retrograde orbit? As I'm about to speak her name, I can feel her cringe. After all, she managed to keep a low profile for four and a half billion years.

But that's all over now. Thanks to a recent visit from the space probe Cassini, her veil of mystery has been lifted. Suddenly, she's in the news.

My loving brother brought the headlines to my attention:

"Oddball Moon Captivates Astronomers"

"Scarred, Cratered Old Surface Points to Checkered Past"

"Saturn's Moon Phoebe: Old, Beaten, and Still Mysterious"

Thanks a lot, bro!

They call her a cosmic vagabond. They think she came from a reservoir of primordial ice chunks way out beyond Neptune. Old, *old* stuff. Building blocks of our solar system. One day—or was it night? Who knows?—she broke from the ice pack, took to the heavenly highways.

Fast forward, a billion years or so:

A planet is born. Stormy young giant, majestic. He strikes one regal pose, then another. But, who is there to see?

Hmmm. A few dozen moons—now, *that* would round out his image. Soon, a goodly circle of admirers. Is there anything… else?

Headline: "Young playboy prince seen with mysterious older woman." And so, captured by Saturn's magnetic personality, Phoebe settles into the court. Well, at the outer edge, anyway. With royal permission to orbit backwards. At a strange, thirty-degree angle. The necessary other, she knows things.

Things about the First Cause. No wonder inquiring minds on planet Earth are excited! How much do you know, Phoebe, and when did you know it? And by the way, who taught you?

The reluctant debutante. Like it or not, she's in the spotlight. Cassini has captured crystal-clear images. These photographs bring new meaning to "she's so ugly she's beautiful."

In the first place, she looks like a sideways skull. Oh, nice! She has a tortured surface, craters within craters, elongated depressions, grooves and ridges. She's oddly dark for a moon, although there *are* patches of brightness… where asteroids have slammed into her.

We look at her endurance, and wonder. The lady is a mother, they think. Some of the cosmic hits she took were so violent that whole chunks of her were blasted away, forming little baby moons that travel with her.

I've had days like that. From the year 1898, when first we spotted her by telescope, Phoebe has fascinated. What is eight hundred million miles, when you really want to know?

So we invented bigger and better telescopes. In 1981, Voyager II sent home fuzzy photographs. And now, spectacular detail from Cassini. Can you imagine? Science plus determination plus tax dollars plus one mere blink of a century gives us the power to shrink great distance. To bring into the sharpest of focus, what? A tiny, oddball moon.

I may look like a chunk of cosmic rubble. But you know what they say about one man's junk! To my Creator, I'm important.

A little beat up by my wanderings, I'm still lovely to him.

A little dark, a little chaotic in my moods—Still, he has a way of teasing out the light.

And, in spite of myself, I smile.

Couple of years later, a headline caught my eye:

Gigantic Surprise Around Saturn
Ring so big 1 billion Earths would fit in it

Pasadena, California—The Spitzer Space Telescope has discovered the biggest but never-before-seen ring around the planet Saturn…The thin array of ice and dust particles lies at the far reaches of the Saturnian system and its orbit is tilted 27 degrees from the planet's main ring plane… the ring is very diffuse and doesn't reflect much visible light, but the infrared Spitzer telescope was able to detect it. Although the ring dust is very cold—minus 316 degrees Fahrenheit—it shines with thermal radiation. The bulk of the ring material starts about 3.7 million miles from the planet and extends outward another 7.4 million miles. Saturn's moon Phoebe orbits within the ring and is believed to be the source of the material ...

Houston Chronicle, October 7, 2009

How can I close without mentioning a few more things?

Christmas morning 2009, when I looked out the back door and beheld an angel on the fence. A red-shouldered hawk, its back to me, breast feathers spread by the sharp cold wind into a nimbus of radiant white. It let me take its picture.

November 2013, Magnolia Cemetery, where my family had just concluded the dedication of three gravestones: for Mother, Daddy, and Uncle Paul. As we stood in silence, a shadow made me look up. High above, circling, were three broad-winged hawks. They gather in circles like that, for long journeys.

Spring 2014: Our Dave, age 32, called to report a strange bird in his yard on Pinchback. It came swooping in on giant wings, then commenced the oddest behavior, stepping about on long legs in a kind of freeze-frame effect: Look away for a minute, look back, and you'll find it's moved forward an inch. This bird suffered Dave to follow it all around the yard, mimicking its movements. We concluded it was a yellow-crowned night heron. Soon after, Dave came to a family gathering, where his heron-step made quite a hit.

Fathers' Day 2014: Our Robert, age 29, arrived from Houston with a bird-report. While bicycling on Braes Bayou, he spotted a duck in the water. By his exquisitely detailed description, we were able to find it in the bird guide. It was none other than the "oddly gooselike" black-bellied whistling-duck. As Robert and I studied the text, Dave did his best approximation of an odd duck with a black belly, whistling. Then, by popular demand, he did his heron-step again.

Were I to write all I know or suppose about every creature I've seen in thirty years on Evangeline, young men included, it would be quite a long book!

Made in the USA
San Bernardino, CA
01 May 2016